Lyra sees the Light

By

CECE SEKULOWICZ

Registered with UK Copyright Service

(Middle Grade Fiction)

Acknowledgements

For many years I had a dream of writing a book, and for most of those many years, did nothing to make that dream into my reality. After years in a job I realised was a) slowly blinding me, b) slowly killing me from the inside out, and c) stopping me from achieving anything, I knew I had to leave. My vision had become a real problem. My life at work became less and less important, and my life outside of work became more important, more pressing. Something urgent was waiting to happen. This book is the product of that pressing matter, and I'm trusting the first in a set of others.

I would like to say a special thank you to my long-time friend and partner Paul, for all the encouragement and useful pointers he gave me on my journey to completing this book. I spent many an evening with him, hunched over my laptop at a table totally unsuitable for the purpose of writing a book, while he worked on his music. I read snippets to him of what I had typed, to see if it made sense. His invaluable advice sought to help my writing become more human and therefore more relatable. I also give thanks to my daughter Rebekah for the videos of accomplished writers, advice on writing technique and her help on issues of layout. A huge thanks to my grandson Che for his observations regarding the length of some of the paragraphs. Well spotted Che! Thank you to my son

Joshua for giving me time to finalise this work, while going through a very difficult time in his life. We really miss you, Stephen. Thanks to the rest of my family (who are with us in spirit or in flesh) and to friends for their feedback and support. Thank you also to Chris Cook for draft after draft of my unfinished book, for his understanding when taking time out to organise my life and also the help he gave me with Amazon. I would also like to thank myself for having the patience, self-belief and determination to work for so long on this vital piece of work, amid so many obstacles that, with help from the Universe and the Most High, I eventually overcame.

After writing the skeleton script in a notebook, I began creating the scene with illustrations, which took my mind away from the day job and helped me to relax. My portfolio of pictures began mounting up and as soon as I had left the workplace for good, I began focusing again, on the storyline. I turned to my trusty laptop at this point and started adding muscle to the skeleton. The scripting went on, until complete, then it was a continuous process of filtering and refining until finally I was happy with the content.

Regarding the illustrations, after some consideration, I decided to use them for a project that would be linked to the book later down the line.

Introduction

This is a middle grade adventure fiction with a twist. Children aged nine and above should be able to read most of the words, and with some thought, begin to understand the message the story is offering. The younger children may benefit from having the story read to them. If a child doesn't understand the meaning of a word, they should ask an adult, who will be able to explain.

The story is written in such a way as to help the reader become accustomed to certain spiritual principles and how they can be used in anyone's life, to better it. The book is suitable for children who wish to enlighten themselves a little, while reading about Lyra's adventures. This first book touches on topics such as: friendship, trust and attraction and goes deeper into knowledge of your Inner Being. It will take you on a journey of self-discovery and help to answer questions you may have already asked yourself.

What begins as an ordinary weekend, turns into an adventure that is far from ordinary. It is the type of adventure most people only dream of having during their childhood, but in the case of the fictional main character, Lyra, she actually does. In Nature Lyra has found something wonderful, she is able to be totally free, untethered by human worries and emotion and she shares that freedom with her best friend Doobey the dog.

CONTENTS

Chapter 1	The weekend begins	Page 4
Chapter 2	Beautiful Souls	Page 7
Chapter 3	Up, up and away	Page 10
Chapter 4	Focusing with your Heart	Page 13
Chapter 5	Mystery of the Green Sanctuary	Page 17
Chapter 6	Golden Structure	Page 20
Chapter 7	The circle of children	Page 23
Chapter 8	Golden Bell treatment	Page 27
Chapter 9	Lyra's challenge begins	Page 33
Chapter 10	Wisdom is given	Page 38
Chapter 11	Journey to Higher Self	Page 40
Chapter 12	Lyra understands the Power within	Page 44
Chapter 13	Returning to the Light	Page 47

Chapter One   The weekend begins

On the surface, Lyra was quite an ordinary sort of girl. She was of medium height for a twelve and a half year old, with dark auburn hair and a mischievous smile. Her brown eyes viewed the world with curiosity and her adventurous character led her to awesome finds, as well as careless accidents. Below the surface though, Lyra had hidden depths that only those closest to her knew about. They were never really spoken about nowadays, just accepted as part of who she is.

Lyra lived with her parents, younger brother Matty, and special friend Doobey the dog, in a town called Beaconsfield. Doobey went everywhere with Lyra, except for school. They had been friends since she was six. Dad had brought him home one evening wrapped in a blanket, and the moment Lyra had seen him, she became besotted. A little border collie pup, with the biggest eyes and wettest nose she had ever seen.

Now Lyra was older, she didn't spend quite so much time with Doobey during the week. She often had homework to do in the evenings, so weekends were a treat for both of them. Lyra loved going out with Doobey. She was fascinated with Nature. Trees, birds, plants, animals, insects, where they lived and how they lived, were of great interest to her. She loved to climb trees and feel their powerful energy, and as she reached the higher branches, report back to Doobey of what she could see.

Their favourite place at the moment was the meadows further down the road, and they went there often. Sometimes they paddled in the stream that ran by the old oak tree. Occasionally they would cross the stream and make their way to the park, visiting the large greenhouses that were full to the brim with tropical fruits and vegetables. They would run like the wind across the meadows, stopping only to catch their breath, as Lyra giggled and Doobey stood panting.

* * * * *

One Saturday morning Lyra woke feeling elated, but didn't know why. She noticed the sunshine peeping through the gap between her bedroom curtains, and felt it was going to be a great day. Jumping out of bed, Lyra pulled back the curtains and looked out of the window. The sun was shining brightly and the tree at the bottom of the garden, was gently swaying in the autumn breeze. She opened the window and took in a few deep breaths, filling her lungs with the cool fresh air. Lyra decided it was a perfect day to spend some time in the meadows with Doobey.

She washed and dressed and pulled on her comfy red trainers. Grabbing her backpack, she ran down the stairs looking for Doobey. Lyra decided she wanted today to be special because the nights were drawing in, the weather was becoming a little chilly, and it was raining more often. Winter was just round the corner so she knew they wouldn't be going out on adventures as often.

Doobey, who had been playing with a ball in the garden, ran to Lyra with his usual bouncy playfulness and gently barked his morning greeting. "Hiya Doobey," Lyra chuckled, rubbing his neck, "are you waiting patiently?" Doobey barked again, "We're going to the meadows in a while, would you like that?" Lyra asked, and Doobey barked yet again, wagging his tail with excitement. It seemed he knew if Lyra was in her jeans, they were going for a long run.

Mum was in the kitchen with Matty who was already eating his breakfast. "Hi mum, hiya Matty," Lyra said with a smile, "We're going to the meadows after breakfast, is that okay?" Mum smiled back, passing her breakfast and told her to be home before teatime. Matty looked at Lyra as though he was going to say something, but no words came out of his mouth and he continued munching on his toast.

She sensed her brother was a little sad and watched as he ate, toast in one hand, a little toy car in the other. Lyra so wanted to take him with them, but he was only six and mum still wouldn't let him go. "Don't worry Lyra," mum said comfortingly, "Tom from next door's coming to play with Matty in a while," she sighed with relief, still wondering why today seemed so special.

In the past Lyra and Doobey had discovered all sorts of things during their outings. Two of their best finds she remembers clearly. They had followed the path of the stream, for what seemed like miles, and just before turning back, had found a mysterious lantern embedded in the stream's muddy bank. After cleaning it up, they had taken it to an antiques shop where they were told it was rare, of exceptional quality, and of Eastern origin. Lyra had profited unexpectedly that day.

On another occasion, while sheltering from a rain shower in one of the greenhouses, Lyra had noticed a small hole in the brickwork below one of the windows. After shining her torch through the hole, it had revealed a tunnel. Too much for Lyra's curiosity, and after some difficulty, she had squeezed through the hole to explore. They made their way towards a light at the other end and found themselves in an empty old house. It had obviously not been lived in for some time. Lyra had told her mum all about it, but the next time they visited the greenhouse, the hole had been bricked up.

Lyra even found something under the grass in their own back garden. Dad had been digging a small area to the side of the house, preparing to make a little pond, but was interrupted with something to do with work. Lyra had continued digging because she had wanted to help, and dad had said it would be okay. After a while and digging deeper, Lyra had discovered a round closure which, with mum's help, they had lifted, and to their amazement, found a spring water well.

* * * * *

Lyra made sandwiches and placed them in her backpack along with a box of biscuits for Doobey, a bottle of water, a towel, and her trusty torch. "Come on Doobey," she announced, "let's get going! Bye mum, see you later!" Mum had no time to answer, Lyra and Doobey had gone. Off they ran, past the little wooden gate at the end of the garden. "Wait for me Doobey!" Lyra shouted, as she ran after him, he was already halfway down the road.

She caught up with him at the meadow gate, and after catching her breath, jumped over the familiar stone wall, landing on the soft mossy grass below. Doobey's tail was wagging furiously, full of the joys of living. He was doing his most favourite thing in the world, with his most favourite person. Off they ran across the wide open meadows, Lyra giggling as she tried to keep up with Doobey, feeling the cool air whizz by her.

They ran on and on, through the long green grass, until Lyra noticed a mound of stones ahead of her. It looked like a very low wall, the type you see around land in the countryside and as she reached it, she jumped. On the other side was a dip and a small hole, which Lyra hadn't seen. She landed awkwardly and stopped abruptly. Something had caught her foot and she was unable to move it.

On realising his playmate was no longer there, Doobey ran back to Lyra. "I've trapped my foot Doobey," she shouted anxiously, looking to see what had happened. Her foot had slipped into the hole, probably made by a rabbit, and was trapped against a rock that was jutting out of the hole. "Look Doobey, I can't move my foot because this rock is holding it in, can you see?" She pointed to it and Doobey moved closer to look, sniffing as he did so.

"You're going to have to dig the hole out so I can wriggle it free," she said, showing him with her hands what she meant. Doobey barked and placed himself in such a way as to use his front legs to kick up the soil. He pawed at the Earth as Lyra held her foot still, but it started becoming a little sore. "Stop Doobey, let's see if it's worked." Lyra leant forward and tried moving her foot, but it was still trapped. She pushed some soil to one side and wriggled her foot again, but it wouldn't budge.

Lyra began to panic, "I can't get my foot out Doobey! The rock's holding it in," and she groaned. Doobey growled at the rock, but that definitely didn't help. She giggled, then wriggled her foot again, but still nothing happened. She tried pushing her other foot against a nearby bush, but it just wouldn't shift. She stood up and looked around, there was no-one in sight to help. Her last resort was to tell Doobey to go and fetch mum, and she was just about to do so, when something alarming happened.

There was a rumble from under the Earth and everywhere started to shake. Both Lyra and Doobey lost their balance and fell over. The hole that Lyra's foot had been trapped in, opened up, and Lyra thankfully pulled it out. The ground rumbled again. Doobey barked anxiously at Lyra, but as he did so, the hole collapsed and they both fell through.

They dropped down and landed with a thud on the ground below. Bits of Earth crumbled above them, shrubs began falling after them, and small rocks that had become loose, fell mercilessly around them. Lyra scrambled for cover near Doobey, sheltering below a large protruding rock, and waited, hoping that nothing awful was happening.

Chapter Two   Beautiful Souls

After what seemed like a few minutes, everything became still again and silence replaced the chaos. Lyra's heart was thumping as she opened her eyes. Doobey was standing over her whining and pushing his nose against her arm. "It's okay Doobey I'm fine, how are you?" she asked, sitting up and rubbing her eyes. She inspected him thoroughly, checking his head, legs, body and paws, she even looked at his tail. Doobey yapped gently a couple of times in a, "I'm fine," kind of way.

She got up, dusting off the Earth and shrubs, stumbling a little as she looked at her foot to see if it was okay. She noticed her ankle was starting to bruise. Looking up, the hole they had fallen through had disappeared and been replaced by a bigger one to the side of them. "What's happened Doobey, where are we?" She asked, and as she viewed the area, the world seemed very different and Lyra felt scared. A large tear rolled down her cheek in despair as Doobey started barking.

Suddenly, amid the commotion, Lyra began to hear music. She wiped her nose as she listened. The music was unlike anything she had ever heard before, and was calming and very comforting. She was caught up in the music and the wonderful feeling it had created, when she heard a voice in her head say, "Do not be afraid Lyra, you are here because you were meant to see our world, and to learn of the wonders that lie within. Will you allow us to show you?"

"Who said that? Doobey, did you hear someone speak?" Lyra squawked, looking around frantically from one direction to another. She could see no-one. Doobey glanced over at Lyra, barked and trotted towards the opening where Light was now streaming through. Lyra followed, limping slightly, still feeling a little stunned and very confused.

She joined Doobey at the opening, stopped and stared in disbelief. What she saw was miles and miles of unfamiliar countryside, spreading out as far as her eyes could see. The meadows seemed to have disappeared and a bright new world had taken its place. Doobey was rooted to the ground, ears standing to attention like two fluffy penguins.

The sky was the brightest shade of red she had ever seen. Thundery skies she had seen in the past, were no comparison. She looked to the right and then to the left, everywhere she looked was covered in a thick blanket of tiny multi coloured flowers. In the distance she could see animals and further into the distance were mountains with what looked like little houses, springing up, here and there.

Lyra and Doobey were staring in stunned amazement, trying to make sense of where they were and what they were seeing, when two figures appeared out of nowhere. Lyra gasped in surprise, backing away a little as she watched the figures move silently closer. They shimmered with brightness as they came towards the confused pair, but Lyra was not afraid, she could feel their energy.

Since a small child, Lyra had been able to feel another person's energy. She knew, without knowing how, when people felt kindly towards her, and when they did not. She was told she was experiencing Auras, the energy that surrounds a person's body. As she grew older, she began to see the colourful energy itself. This helped Lyra stay safe. She knew immediately these unusual beings were gentle.

They moved gracefully forward and stopped in front of Lyra and Doobey. The smaller, female figure smiled as she bowed her head and opened her hands in friendship. She was wearing a long flowy garment which appeared to be made from a delicate blue material, which on closer inspection were tiny woven feathers and her golden hair almost touched the ground. The male figure wore a similar garment, made from a heavier red material. His messy brown hair was much shorter and his jolly face beamed as he looked at them. Lyra noticed a gentleness surrounding her.

The male figure bowed as he lifted his hands to his head. Lyra heard words in her mind again, saying, "Do not be afraid, I am the one who spoke. I am Dimaryp and," he signalled to his female companion, "I am Laeh," she said, "and this land is called Airumel." They bowed their heads again and placed their right hand across their heart. Lyra curtsied politely, "Erm, I am Lyra and he's Doobey, but where are we and how do you know my name?"

"You are in a world very different to your own Lyra, deep below the surface of the Earth," Dimaryp replied. "Deep below the surface!! What do you mean? ... How is that possible?" Lyra gushed as she looked around anxiously. "Didn't we just fall down a hole? And I can hear you talking but your mouths aren't moving, how is **that** possible?"

"Do not be troubled Lyra," Dimaryp said gently, "we are speaking to you from our mind, but you **will** hear what we say," he explained. "You mean you're telepathic?" Lyra asked curiously, "We learnt about that last term at school. I didn't know if it was really possible." Dimaryp agreed that it is a form of telepathy, "We are aware of what another is thinking Lyra and we can transmit thoughts, words and images through our mind to yours." Lyra gasped in surprise.

Laeh moved closer and asked, "May I look at your foot Lyra?" They were aware Lyra and Doobey could have hurt themselves during the collapse, so she inspected Lyra, and then Doobey. She stood opposite them and used her hand to scan their bodies, searching for any injuries. "You are both whole," she said, "but your ankle is bruising Lyra, may I attend to it for you?"

Feeling puzzled and curious at the same time, Lyra sat down on a rock. Laeh rubbed her hands together briskly and held them out over the area that was turning purple. She closed her eyes and moved her hands slowly, back and forth over the area for a few seconds. Gradually the bruising faded and the discomfort Lyra had been feeling disappeared.

"Wow, thank you Laeh that's amazing, how did you do that?" Laeh explained that she had used a healing method similar to Reiki to restore the vessels in Lyra's foot. "When your body is hurt by injury, or by worry, the energy within your body starts to block. Reiki helps to heal the hurt by moving the blocked energy. When energy flows freely, your body becomes balanced and works the way it is supposed to work," she said. Lyra's mind was now racing with questions.

Who are they, she thought, and **how** did they get here, in fact, how did **we** get here? Are there others? And how **do** they know my name? Without a word, Dimaryp began answering. "Laeh is my partner," he said smiling at her. "We are here as the Yin and Yang, to show you how Balance and Harmony exist below the surface of the Earth. There are many of us, and we all live alongside Nature, hurting nothing and respecting everything." Lyra smiled, it sounded like her kind of world.

"We are unsure exactly of how we got here, we were in a type of trance, but we know Nature helped. We are able to travel backwards and forwards inside the Earth and outside across the surface. We wish to show as many children as possible that they are the helpers of humanity. The qualities many children possess, such as honesty, curiosity and determination, are needed on Earth right now. They will help heal the Earth and bring peace back to mankind. You are one of those children Lyra."

She gasped again wondering what Dimaryp could possibly mean. Here to help mankind? How could a girl like her help heal the Earth? She wanted to know more. They looked at each other and smiled, "Lyra," Laeh said gently, "children understand things that most adults do not understand. As a child grows into an adult on Earth, they learn to stop asking questions, their innocent curiosity is lost, they follow the crowd and are expected to accept things the other adults accept. Children are different, they are open to anything and love to know more.

You are blessed because your parents are interested in things that are still seen as out of the ordinary, frowned upon even. For example, holistic medicine, off-grid living, vegan food, life force energy and also the way they are raising you and your brother."

Lyra thought about how her classmates teased her because she loved to eat raw vegetables, especially cabbage, and how they worried so much about the latest trends. "Does that mean my parents are weird?" Lyra asked, remembering something that had been said. "It means they are more open to new ideas Lyra, and will support your ideas, so long as they are sensible," Laeh informed her. "They are raising you to think for yourself and to be individual."

Lyra was fascinated, she continued, "Why is it nobody speaks about all of you and this beautiful world?" She was amazed that no-one had ever told her about it. "Few of your people know about Airumel and the people that do, want to keep it to themselves. They think by not speaking about it, we will remain their secret, but it will cause pain. Humans need to know of us, we are your Ancestors." Laeh replied.

"Wow … that's deep, and you're still here!" Lyra blurted out. "But the opening ….?" remembering her recent painful experience, "Where has the opening gone, how do we get back to the surface?" Dimaryp explained that the hole they fell through was not an entrance, or an exit to their world. The ground collapsed because it had become weak. The maze of rabbit warrens and mole habitats in that area, just below the surface, had left the ground unstable.

"It was waiting for **you** Lyra, that is why the rock wouldn't let you go," Dimaryp said, winking at Lyra, "the rock sends its apologies for hurting your foot." Lyra frowned, then chuckled, "Apology accepted," she said, in a 'Great Aunt' sort of way. "After the collapse," Dimaryp continued, "you and Doobey made a mystical journey to us." Lyra was amazed and didn't understand any of it, and even though she felt a deep urge to know more, she also felt a little lost and confused.

"Do not be sad Lyra, we will make certain you return home safely when you are ready to leave," Laeh assured her. She felt well acquainted to Lyra, having observed her since birth. Laeh saw someone with a great love for life, caring enough to look after it and knowing that something would be affected, if she didn't. She did find Lyra to be a little careless with her own life though, which she knew Lyra would soon grow out of.

"Would you like to see our world Lyra, or would you rather we took you back to the surface?" Dimaryp asked. Lyra gazed past the two of them as she considered the question, then she looked at Doobey whose tail was wagging vigorously. "I may get home late, won't my mum be wondering where we are?" She asked politely. "When you return to your world," Dimaryp explained, "it will be just as it was when you left. No time will have passed, because here, there is no time."

Chapter Three   Up, up and away

Lyra smiled as she bounced up and down on the balls of her feet, clapping her hands. She decided this was an adventure she couldn't possibly miss out on, "I would love to see more of your world," she answered excitedly and giggled as Doobey trotted around her with his tongue hanging out.

Dimaryp put his hands to his head again, and a small flying craft appeared. It looked like a large copper cup, with no handle. The craft hovered in the air, as if awaiting orders of where to go, then settled on the ground close to where they were standing.

"Where are we going first?" Lyra asked curiously. "We are going way over there," Laeh said, pointing to a mountain range in the distance, "We can sit comfortably and observe, so please feel free to ask us anything you wish." Lyra smiled, stroking Doobey's head a little nervously, as Laeh directed them into the craft. "It is okay Lyra, you will be quite safe," she said.

Lyra had never seen anything quite like the copper flying cup before. Inside there were two seats, one at either end of the craft. She climbed in and sat down and Doobey jumped up onto the seat next to her. Laeh and Dimaryp moved effortlessly into the craft and settled on the seat opposite.

The first thing Lyra noticed was the lack of controls, no steering wheel, no brakes, nothing, so she asked how the craft was able to move. "It is controlled by us Lyra. We use our mind to rotate the air at superfast speed. This moves us up, down, or side to side, very effective for smaller crafts." Lyra thought about it, then realising the craft came to Dimaryp in the same way Doobey comes to her when she shouts, it did sort of make sense.

Dimaryp continued, "We have larger crafts too, but they are powered differently, by a certain type of crystal. None of the crafts are powered by harmful gases, like in your world." Lyra was impressed, imagining her world free from pollution. It would be so wonderful she thought, the air would be so fresh and clean for everyone to breathe.

The flying cup lifted upwards off the ground like a silent helicopter, then began moving swiftly through the air. Doobey looked coyly over the side, while Lyra held onto the seat. She thought it felt a little like the time she was seated on the big wheel at the fairground with her dad, way above the crowd. She looked up into the sky. It was so different to the sky she was used to, calm and red with no Sun anywhere to be seen.

"Where is the Sun, oh, but do you have a Sun?" she asked, wondering if that could be possible, inside the Earth. "Yes we do and you will see it sooner or later," Laeh replied. "Sooner or later?" Lyra giggled. "It does not have a set motion Lyra. It comes and goes as it pleases, and sometimes plays games with us, shining in one place and then appearing way off a moment later. It can move very quickly." Imagine that, Lyra thought, how awesome to have a Sun that plays games with you.

Feeling more confident now, she edged her way to the side, still holding the seat, and looked over. Way below she saw children floating around just above the ground, moving as though they were swimming through the air, others appeared to be playing some kind of instruments, while two little girls were dancing.

Lyra marvelled at the unusually coloured, familiar looking animals. She saw a large green lion with a bright orange mane, and there were others drinking from a bubbling pink river nearby. Further away she saw a group of purple giraffes gathered around a tree filled with multi-coloured birds.

"We call them noils," Laeh instructed as she watched Lyra studying the lions. "And the lofty purple animals are effarigs. If you look closely in that tree, you will see some little pink tibbars hiding between the leaves. Can you see them?" she asked, pointing towards an inky blue tree. Lyra peered at the tree for a while and after careful inspection, suddenly realised, what she had thought were just clusters of leaves, actually contained little pink rabbits.

Lyra surveyed the land, using her hands as pretend binoculars. She noticed what looked like a brown and cream horse. "Is that a zebra Laeh?" She asked. "Ah yes the arbez, they are very similar to zebras, the only difference is their markings." As they spoke, a flock of exotic sounding birds, with crested heads and multi coloured wings flew over the copper cup. They made a sound like castanets being played for a flamenco dancer. Lyra giggled and waved as she watched the unusual birds fly over.

On they travelled in the flying cup, dipping and hovering now and again, to get a better look. She noticed a large modern building covered in geometric patterns, which seemed to have no door, then groups of enormous crystals that sprang up out of the ground, like fountains frozen in time. There were winding pathways and tall columns glistening and shining as they moved silently on through the sky, and for a moment, she thought she glimpsed a pyramid.

The trees and their branches were shades of silver and blue displaying pretty pink leaves. The golden vines which grew around some of the larger trunks, gave the appearance of a helter-skelter ride. Lyra wondered what the seasons were inside the Earth as Nature appeared to be in the early stages of spring. "The weather stays the same here Lyra, warm and mild and so do the seasons, everything grows healthily, lasts as long as it lasts, then repeats." Laeh answered helpfully. Lyra nodded.

After a while the flying cup settled about half way up a gently sloping mountainside. "Wow the colours here are so intense, look at the grass Doobey!" Lyra shouted in excitement!" She viewed the scenery as she clambered out of the craft a little carelessly, tripping over a clump of tangerine grass. "Everything is so bright and colourful," she observed, tickling Doobey's neck playfully as they walked.

Before long they found a spot between some sweet smelling bushes, so Lyra sat down and made herself comfortable. She gazed around this strange, new world in awe. The beautiful countryside was everywhere she looked. Some of the houses were much closer now, she could even see the artistry on the outside walls. There were sculptured figures of animals, and children with happy faces. It looked like they had been moulded into the building. Elegant designs were carved into the wooden doors and some of the roofs had shrubs growing out of them.

Lyra noticed there was no concrete to be seen, anywhere. There were no walls, fences, or barriers of any description. "We do not need boundaries Lyra, we respect each other's space completely. We make sure we have room to come and go as we please. We do not hoard land either, there is more than enough for everyone and each family has a good sized, equal portion."

Looking across at them, Lyra sighed wistfully, "Your world is different to ours. It seems so calm and orderly, but I suppose you knew I was thinking that …. Is it fascinating reading minds?" Doobey barked as Laeh replied, "Yes Lyra, we all know what each other is thinking. It makes everything so much easier than using words, those things can be very misleading."

Lyra wondered if she could cope with hearing everyone's thoughts. "We put our mind to one thing at a time, so usually we only hear one thing at a time. It is not as difficult as it sounds Lyra. We have learnt how to free our mind, so it is not full up with worries about the past and doubts about the future. We think around the moment we are in. That allows us to concentrate fully on what we are doing in that moment." Lyra smiled, seeing the sense in that.

She pointed to the columns and then to the pathways, stating how beautiful they were. "They are all made from crystals," Laeh replied, "there are hundreds of them, some even make their way to the surface where humans find them. They are very powerful, so powerful we use them to light our cities. Crystals are part of the eco system, as are the rivers and fountains but **everything** exists because of the Great Sun, like in the sky above your world Lyra."

Laeh remembered a story she had been told as a youngster, by her guardian. It was of a time when Angelic beings had created huge crystals and placed them in caves, deep within the Earth and below the rivers and sea beds. Laeh explained how these ancient crystals had broken into small pieces, but still possess the same power and wisdom today. "Each crystal has its own unique property, but they all give the protection, peace and focus needed in daily living." Lyra listened with great interest.

"The crystal columns keep the energy connected, they work in a similar way to electricity pylons across the Earth, energising whenever needed. The blue crystal pathways lead to healing chambers inside the sanctuaries. Some humans use them to remove suffering in their body. There is one over there," Dimaryp said, as he pointed towards a strange green building in the distance.

"So you mean other people come here from my world?" Lyra asked curiously. "Yes Lyra, sometimes. If a human needs to be healed, they come here while they are asleep, in their dream," Laeh explained. Lyra was confused. How can a person visit the healing chambers in their sleep? How can their body be healed, if they are having a dream? "Would you like to look inside?" Dimaryp asked.

Lyra wondered again if **she** was dreaming. Is this really possible? Maybe she had been hit on the head by a rock and was imagining all of this. Or perhaps they never really fell through the Earth at all, but they had just gone home and she was now in bed, fast asleep. Dimaryp interrupted her thoughts, "You are not dreaming my dear and you were not hit on the head by a rock. You are here with us, in a world deep below the surface of the Earth. We have lived this way for centuries."

Chapter Four   Focusing with your Heart

"Are you very old?" Lyra asked, opening her backpack and getting Doobey a biscuit. "Oh yes Lyra we are **very** old," Laeh said, "My life as Laeh began around the time of Christopher Columbus." Lyra's eyes widened, and her mouth fell open as she studied them carefully. But they look so young she thought, they don't look any older than my mum and dad. She tried not to stare … or think, in case they heard her.

"Don't you get old … or sick, and don't you," she considered the question carefully, but no, she had to ask, "well … don't you … how can you be so old? Don't you die?" Lyra asked. She didn't want to sound rude, but she knew from her history lessons that Columbus died over 500 years ago.

"We do not get old Lyra, and we very rarely become sick. This is because of the way we live," Dimaryp said, smiling at Lyra's innocence. "Death as you call it though is usually very different. When we reach a certain level of spiritual growth, we transform into a higher state of being. It is like upgrading."

Lyra listened intently, keen to know more. She decided it would be interesting to go and explore the sanctuary Dimaryp had pointed out. She opened her backpack again and took out the sandwiches. "Would you like one of these?" Lyra asked politely, a little unsure of what their answer would be, "I made them myself, there's avocado and cucumber in them …" Laeh thanked Lyra, but explained that food was unnecessary, so they rarely ate it.

"How do you live without food?" Lyra asked, taking another bite of her sandwich. "Our bodies, or vessels, are not like yours Lyra," Laeh explained, "they are not carbon based, as yours are, they are crystalline based, so we gain all our energy from the Sun. We are only apparent to you in this moment because we wish you to see us."

Lyra was fascinated. "You mean you can become invisible!?" she asked excitedly, "Yes, if we do not wish to show ourselves," Dimaryp said. "Oh wow!!" Lyra exclaimed, almost choking on her sandwich. "How do you do that?" They told her it was a process that is based on the 'mind over matter' theory, but requires focus and practice.

Lyra sat quietly, munching on her sandwich, deep in thought. After she had finished, she gave Doobey another biscuit and got up. "Can we see the sanctuary now?" she asked eagerly, she wanted to see the place where bodies can be healed in a dream. Laeh and Dimaryp stood up, "Of course, it is our pleasure to take you there," they replied.

The four of them set off down the mountainside until they reached the blue quartz path. Doobey ran on ahead to investigate. A group of enormous butterflies flew slowly by, gently wafting their large blue wings up and down. Lyra gasped in surprise as she felt the energy of their Auras. It was clear and very bright and their wings made a type of 'phwooo' noise as they moved.

She could see the sanctuary clearly now. It was an old stone building in a beautiful shade of emerald green. The roof appeared to be a type of thatch, similar to the cottages near where she lived, but again, the thatch had different coloured shrubs growing out of it. There were windows along both sides, and below them grew purple vines, stretching the length of the building, creating a flame-like appearance.

The crystal pathway came to an end near the sanctuary door. Before entering, Lyra stopped to stroke a pink horse, who seemed to be in deep conversation with a turquoise turtle. The horse shook its head and neighed at Lyra in a, "Good day Lyra" sort of way. Lyra chuckled, "Good day to you both," she said, before heading over to a fountain she had spotted, to take a closer look. It stood out against the bright red sky, glowing with the energy within. Doobey stopped chasing the butterflies and ran over to join Lyra.

"The fountain itself is made from different types of crystals and the tiers are made of gold," Laeh pointed out. Lyra looked closely at the water, seeing it was different in appearance to ordinary water. It had a pinkish tinge to it and the large drops of water moved unusually. "I sometimes come here to meditate," Laeh said, "when there is not a Soul around. The water soothes me into a wonderful frame of mind."

Lyra watched as the crystal water gently danced out of the spout, almost thoughtfully, glistening like pink diamonds for a second or two, then tumbling over the edge and slowly settling in the crystal water below. "This is so pretty, and **so** unusual," Lyra observed, hypnotised by the fountain's twinkling water. She was woken from her trance-like state when she heard Doobey barking.

He was jumping playfully into the air as more huge butterflies wafted by. "You can't jump that high," Lyra giggled. Laeh explained that the flutterbies are the noils special friends. "The flutterbies love to tease the lazy noils. They see Doobey and wonder what he is, there are no dogs in Airumel, just wolves." Lyra nodded, still giggling, and tingling from the flutterbies energy, as she followed Laeh into the sanctuary.

Once inside, she looked around at its charmingly simple appearance. Its organic walls and ceiling were a little bumpy and a floor covering similar to seagrass rustled underfoot as she walked. The framework of the building was made from beautifully crafted wood and to the right of her was a raised platform covered in heart shaped flowers.

Lyra took a deep breath in and smiled, the fragrance reminded her of one of her mum's favourite perfumes. "Yes that is a wonderful aroma Lyra, it pleases my sense of smell also." Lyra nodded. "They are petals from a Pilut plant. We replenish that area as soon as the fragrance disappears because we like to keep things fresh. It is lovely to be greeted by a sweet smell, is that not so Lyra?" She nodded again in agreement.

There were plants around the sanctuary that were growing out of the Earth, through the floor, and straight up the walls. The plants were being allowed to grow naturally, even inside the building. Lyra decided that allowing plants to grow just where they want to grow, is truly respecting Nature. "That plant looks just like a fountain," she said observing a very unusual blue plant. "Yes Lyra, we call it the Mimic plant. There are a few of them, but this is the first time one has actually mimicked a fountain." Lyra chuckled, so it's looking like that on purpose, she thought.

Studying the arched, glassless window, she noticed an unusual pattern had been worked into the framework. It was similar to the patterns on the houses she had just seen. Looking around the room, she could see exposed wood in certain areas. Dimaryp explained to Lyra that the wood was the skeleton of the building and was layered with a natural material. "In your world it is called Cob," he said. "A great material to build with, and most of the houses here are made from it.

Cob is clay, sand and straw, easy to find in Nature, dug with the hands and mixed with the feet, messy, but fun. It lasts a very long time if cared for properly. In your world Lyra, when the weather is cold outside, a cob structure will be warm inside, and when it is warm outside, the structure will be cool inside. Cob can repel insects and stop mould growth, due to the smooth hard outer layer that is protected with a lime wash. Buildings like these are very friendly to the environment."

Lyra believed a time would soon come when more people would choose to live in houses like these. Her parents had spoken about it in the past and again more recently. Last year they had visited a community who were building their own houses and then living in them. They were growing their own fruit and vegetables and some kept chickens for their eggs and goats for their milk. Mum and dad had been very interested in all of it.

Lyra was distracted when she spotted a bookstand full of old books. Most of the books were about the Earth and the Stars. "Are you interested in Stars Lyra?" Laeh asked. She thought about the question and for a moment began daydreaming of a time when she was a small child. She saw herself lying on the grass in the back garden, gazing up at the sky, in awe of its vastness, and as she witnessed the millions of stars, wondered if the sky came to an end, and if it did, where, and what came after?

Lyra decided around that point in her life, at about the age of five, just after her grandpa had passed away suddenly, that life did **not** end there. She decided there was much more to life than that, and that we don't just live, then die. For ever and ever? No, that was definitely not possible in Lyra's mind. Lyra decided that evening the sky did go on forever, which made her think that people did too.

She stopped daydreaming and answered, "Yes, I love to read about the Stars, and the Earth, it's really interesting." She walked over to the bookstand to take a closer look. "May I touch one of the books," she asked politely, "they do look very old, and that one is dropping to bits!" Dimaryp agreed and moved over to where she was standing. He explained that she was free to read any of the books, but there was no need to touch them, as he could open any without touching.

"Oh, okay Dimaryp can I see that one?" she asked eagerly, and pointed to a thick silver bound book entitled, 'Atlantis, how we made our escape.' Laeh smiled at Dimaryp as he focused on the book. After a moment, as if by magic, it turned and slid onto its back, then the cover swung open. Lyra watched in amazement, "Ooooo, how did you do that?" she asked, clapping her hands. "I would love to be able to do that!"

Laeh explained to Lyra that she **could** do it, with practice and self-belief, "It is a matter of focusing on just one thing," she said practically. "You should focus **all** of your thought, onto the object you wish to move. The key is to think about nothing else, except moving the object. Why don't you try closing the book?" Laeh asked.

Lyra giggled nervously, thinking Laeh was joking and doubted herself immediately. "I don't really know how to think about just one thing," she said, feeling disappointed, "my mind talks to me, even when I don't want it to, it just keeps chattering away." Laeh and Dimaryp were fully aware of how so many humans do not practise Mindfulness, so Laeh spoke out an exercise, to help 'train' the mind to focus.

"Sit somewhere quiet and close your eyes, this will cut out distractions. Think about just one thing. Picture this thing in your mind's eye. Look at it, see its shape and colour. Keep your focus on it and every time your mind wanders, which it will to begin with, bring it back to the object. Mindfulness is being aware of where we are and what we are doing, in that moment, without reacting or being overwhelmed."

Dimaryp sensed a feeling of defeat coming from Lyra, "Do not give in Lyra. Do not be sad. Humans do that too often, then they lose sight of their goal. Remember, you are bringing about something new. You must believe that it **will** happen. Have Faith in your **own** ability to move the object, have Faith in your power to do anything, but feel the Joyfulness of doing it, **before** it is done."

They understood how difficult it must be for Lyra. How this must sound to someone who has so little knowledge of these teachings. To someone who knows nothing about the mysteries of the Universe, mysteries Lyra would probably call, magic. "You are about to do something that is possible. Believe in what you are doing Lyra. Tell yourself, I know I can do this. Do not listen to any other thought. Concentrate, and you will succeed."

Lyra looked at Laeh in amazement and stood in thought for a while, then she nodded her head, frowned with determination and said, "Yes, let me try." She took a deep breath and stared at the book. After a few moments Lyra glanced at Laeh and with a very serious voice she said, "I think I'll try turning a page, it weighs less than the cover." Laeh shook her head and reminded Lyra to focus back to the book.

Lyra bowed her head and was still for a moment. She emptied her mind of any thoughts she was having and then when she felt unburdened and free, she looked again at the book. She pursed her lips and narrowed her eyes and focused on the book. She noticed again it was large, so probably quite heavy, then she saw the pages were faded and a little tatty around the edges.

Her mind began to wander, did she need to go into some kind of trance? Pictures suddenly started popping into her mind, first the flying cup and then the children and … "No Stop!!" She shouted at her mind, "Be Quiet! Stay with the page!" She giggled at herself and after looking over at Laeh, shuffled her feet, cleared her throat and focused on the book, yet again.

A few quiet minutes passed by this time, in which she managed to hold one thought. It was a quiet she knew, a little like the way you feel when you first wake up after sleeping, peaceful and drowsy. As Lyra held onto the one thought, the thought of lifting the page, she became powerful without realising. This **was** 'Mind over Matter.' She stared at the page, breathing steadily and concentrating deeply.

Slowly, the page Lyra was focusing on, gradually started to move …. Lyra was so surprised she lost her focus and the page stopped moving. "Well done Lyra, you did it!" they said with praying hands. Lyra looked over at them in surprise, she wasn't sure what she had done, and, gazing back at the page, could see no answer there either.

"But what did I do?" she asked. "You were fully focused Lyra … and the page began to move. It only stopped moving, when you lost your focus. You lost your focus, because you didn't believe you were actually making it move." She was stunned and couldn't help wondering if they had helped. "We did not help you Lyra, that would have been cheating, and what would that have proved?" they answered together.

Laeh explained that with practise she would be able to focus past the excitement of starting, to actually keeping the page lifted. "Would that work in my world too?" Lyra asked hopefully. "Yes of course, if you concentrate in the same way," Dimaryp said, "and Lyra, the weight of an object is not important. It is the strength of your mind's focus that is important, and knowing in your heart that you can do it."

Chapter Five   Mystery of the Green Sanctuary

Dimaryp decided to explain something to Lyra he felt she should know. "You have a word in your language Lyra, the word is 'hope'. We never use that word because it sounds like possible failure. Hope just brings more hope. Try using the word 'trust' instead, it sends out a stronger message, it sounds more successful. Trust brings more trust, which brings belief it will happen. Do you understand Lyra?" Lyra was nodding slowly, listening along with great interest.

"Humans make things so difficult for themselves," Laeh continued. "The Universe works for each one of us like magic. The Universe brings about the things we think about, so, it is important not to change our mind about what we want. If we keep changing our mind, we are sending out mixed messages to the Universe. The more time spent on our thoughts, the more real they become, so it is vitally important we think only about the things we wish to receive, nothing else."

Lyra smiled, as young as she was, she saw great wisdom in what she was being taught. She nodded in agreement and looked again at the open book. The writing was different to any book they had at home, or at school, or any library book she had ever seen. The letters were curly and written in a faded green ink. She read the two open pages. It spoke of a battle that had taken place on the surface of Earth many years ago.

"I would love to read all of that book, but I can't touch it can I, and …" Lyra's voice trailed off. "You think you will not see us again?" They asked together. Lyra looked over at them. "You are welcome to return whenever you want," Dimaryp said, as he focused again and closed the silver bound book.

"It is important to remember one thing above all else," Laeh began protectively, "Whatever you do, do it through your heart. Let your heart filter your thoughts, words and actions, it will help you to choose carefully the good things only, you wish to keep. By doing this, you will see the best outcome for everyone." Lyra nodded slowly and stood for a while reflecting on what she had learnt.

* * * * *

"Is this where the healing takes place?" She asked after a while. "Follow me," Dimaryp replied as he walked towards a heavy wooden door. It was covered in an intricate display of circles and squares. Someone had skilfully carved the design into the wood. Dimaryp focused on the door for a moment, it opened slowly and they followed him into a corridor. On either side of the corridor were three more doors. Lyra watched as one of the doors opened, obeying Dimaryp's silent command.

He stood back as Doobey entered the room, sniffing his way along the floor, followed by Lyra and Laeh. The first thing Lyra noticed were the bright shiny walls, she had never seen anything like them before. They glistened in the light as she turned to view the awesome sight. The walls looked as though they were made from jewels. "They are a mixture of gold, silver, copper and brass," Laeh said, "they help with the healing process." Lyra looked eagerly round the room, her eyes darting from one thing to another.

She saw more strange looking plants that had grown up through the floor. Lyra thought one plant looked like a bonfire, its thick purple leaves resembled flames and were tipped with delicate red flowers. An attractive green border, similar to an Aztec design, had been painted around the arched window. A small square tree was growing at the other end of the room. She blinked at it a few times, but no, she wasn't seeing things, it was definitely square. In front of that was a low crystal table, glowing near Doobey. Lyra walked over to the table and touched it.

"That is where the healing takes place," Laeh said, observing Lyra's interest. "Please tell me how it works," she asked, baffled how someone could be healed there, while sleeping in their bed. "A Higher Mind may bring a Soul here while dreaming. The walls unite with the crystal table, and together they draw out the toxins in the body. Upon awakening, the body feels fresh and energised." Lyra gasped and a tear of joy rolled down her cheek. She thought of the miracles this room could perform.

She turned again and spotted another fountain through the arched window. It seemed to be made from clear quartz crystal. She knew about those crystals because she had one. Mum had bought it on her tenth birthday, after falling from a tree and breaking her leg. She had taken Lyra to a very interesting little shop in the town, to choose the one she liked the best, telling her it would be helpful in relieving the pain.

Lyra pulled the necklace out from under her jumper to show them. "That fountain, is it clear quartz like this?" she asked, pointing through the window, "my mum got it for me when I broke my leg," she explained. "Yes Lyra, and did it ease your pain?" Laeh asked gently. Thinking carefully, Lyra decided it had helped, because soon after she started wearing it, she had stopped needing to use the cold compress at night.

"Are there any more sanctuaries?" Lyra asked. "Yes, there are others," Laeh replied. "Are they for healing too?" she asked, dropping the chain back down the inside of her jumper. "Yes in a way Lyra, they are less about illness though and more about Strength and Focus. One of them is for cleansing Auras, balancing Chakras and strengthening the Third Eye, the Eye that sees way beyond looking. We call it the Pyramid of Light." Lyra nodded, thinking maybe that was what she had seen earlier.

"The Temple of Essence, a very powerful place, takes us back to how we once were, innocent, open, good-natured, curious and spontaneous. In that state of being, while having nothing to compare, we see everything the way a young child sees, as though it was the very first time. This makes it simple to know everything properly because there is no memory, so there is no comparison."

Lyra stood for a while absorbing the information. "Why don't we have places like those on Earth? Wouldn't they be helpful to us?" she asked. Dimaryp laid a comforting hand on her shoulder and said, "Do not be sad Lyra, humans will catch up. There are some, who must still learn that power over others is holding them back. One by one they will realise, the only way forward, is to stop being greedy and to Love each other, unconditionally." Lyra sighed, imagining the contentment on Earth.

"Okay, well I think I understand Chakras, but Source?" she asked, "To be clear, Chakras are energy centres in your body. You have seven of them, starting at the base of your spine, moving upwards in sections, to the top of your head. In a healthy, grounded human, the Chakras give the right balance of energy to the Mind, Body and Soul, bringing you harmony. Source my child, is where we all began. It is the beginning of everything. Some call it the Most High, the Source of who you really are." Lyra was fascinated.

"There is a **huge** tree, not far from here where Annie, our Oracle lives. She has mastered the art of receiving messages from Source," Dimaryp told Lyra. "Really! What kind of messages?" Lyra asked excitedly. "All kinds of messages Lyra, but they will always be about the person she is with. The Universe works with Source, they know your dreams. They also knows what you are ready to learn. The Oracle will reveal things that can help you make the best of your life."

Lyra's eyes widened as she listened intently, drawn to what she was hearing, imagining herself in conversation with The Oracle. "Would it be possible to meet with The Oracle?" she asked politely. Laeh smiled looking over at Dimaryp as he replied, "Yes of course my child. Our Oracle lives in a treehouse not too far from here. If you can find her, she will help you find yourself." Lyra was puzzled, what did he mean, find myself?

"We all have a gift Lyra, something we can do really well," Laeh explained, "Some have more than one. They are given freely when we are born. It is yours to use whenever you desire. When you use your gift, you excel at what you do, this brings Joy to your life and allows others to feel at Peace when they are near you. This is most important in your world right now. The more humans who feel at Peace, the more humanity will be healed."

"The Oracle knows you, by feeling you, wherever you are, and she is far older than either of us," Dimaryp continued. "The messages come in the moment, with whoever she is with. She puts the messages into order and translates them back to you. She will help you to dive deep into yourself, entering a different realm, then explaining things that will help you to grow."

"The Oracle can speak about anything. She knows you are here, but will only help if you can find her," Laeh said. "It means the Universe wishes you to know your destiny in this way." Lyra was inspired, she wanted to prove she could do it, "If Doobey can come and it's not too far, I'd love to!"

A thought appeared, "Laeh, there aren't any monsters are there?" even though she thought she sounded rather silly, but just wanted to be sure. "Not at all," came Laeh's reply, "There are different animals, many like the animals on the surface, but they are all tame. We play with the noils, the children sometimes ride on their backs. They are very gentle creatures."

"We do not hunt animals, and animals do not hunt us, they are our friends, and we are theirs. All the animals are vegetarian," Dimaryp explained. "Hunting is very primitive. Nature is highly advanced here. Some of the plants can talk. Some of the trees can walk, but you will discover these things the longer you are here." Lyra's eyebrows raised in wonder. She sat pondering again. She had never heard anything like this before.

* * * * *

They set off down the mountainside. As Lyra walked, she considered the contrast between the buildings in Airumel. Some were fashioned by the builder's hands, some, like those she had seen earlier, were angular and very twenty first century looking. She ran on ahead to catch up with Doobey, over a hilly piece of land, and as she caught up, she noticed something gleaming a little way off.

It appeared to be a shelter made of gold. It was ornate and very majestic looking. "What is it used for?" She asked with curiosity, touching the smooth, golden floor as she stepped inside. There were two long seats, and at the opposite end, a pile of large comfy cushions. "Really, a lovely place to relax and observe the wonder of Creation," Laeh explained. "It is made entirely of Golden Healer Quartz, so extremely soothing to the Soul." Lyra nestled herself amongst the cushions as Laeh and Dimaryp sat down on one of the long seats.

Chapter 6   Golden structure

Lyra lay there for a while, gazing up at the clear red sky. She inhaled, tasting the warm fresh air, making little clicky sounds with her mouth as she did so. Doobey ran off and began bouncing around, yapping at some birds as they flew overhead. She felt a calmness descend upon her, it was very peaceful and while she lay amongst the cushions, she felt herself let go of any small worries.

As they sat, Dimaryp began to tell Lyra about the differences between inner Earth and surface Earth. "Our world is not clogged up with noise, traffic and pollution," he said. "Your world used to be the same as ours, but it has changed. It is now ruled by money. Inner Earth has no money, there is no need for it."

"Each family has a large portion of land and they build their home on that land," Leah explained, joining in. "This gives each family space to move around freely. Most people on the surface who live in cities, live in buildings far too close to each other, many, as you have seen, literally on top of each other, and are forced into spending a big part of their adult lives working, to pay just to live there."

Lyra's mind drifted, she was in London with school, aged ten. She remembered watching the people. Most of them were rushing somewhere, some pushing in, others walking straight across your path. There seemed to be very little patience or consideration, except for one kind lady. She had helped them find their way back to the bed and breakfast they were staying in after she and a classmate had got lost, separated from the group while looking for gifts. Laeh did praying hands and continued.

"It is the indigenous people of your world, who still live off the land. Natives of Africa, North America, Australia, New Zealand and parts of Asia, they still live the same way their Ancestors did, in tune with the Earth and the whole of Nature. Our lives are very similar. We have no holidays, they are not necessary. We live simple lives based on integrity and growth and is fruitfully rewarded."

"Fruitfully rewarded?" Lyra asked. "Yes, by working together, each sharing your own gift, you reap the reward of whatever it is you are creating. There is patience and co-operation so things flow and come together with ease. Whoever works alongside you … family, friends, community, have a share in whatever is produced. Nothing is lost and we have fun, and learn, while we are producing.

In your world, many humans work for people who do not share their profits. Those who own or manage their business have become greedy, they take more than their fair share, so there is less for everyone else." Lyra nodded slowly, she was beginning to see how it made sense to work for yourself.

"Too many poor communities across the Earth have little or nothing to eat, nowhere to live, some, not even a bed to sleep on. Those with spare cash get a taste of freedom, once or twice a year, in the form of a holiday. The rest of the year is spent working, or studying in order to work, just so they have enough money to continue living like that. Where is the enjoyment?" Lyra shook her head in dismay.

"We make everything we use and exchange between ourselves and the other communities. There is value in everything because we do not put a price on it. Everything we make has a use and therefore valuable to the one who wants it. I could make a beautiful crystal lantern, and exchange it for a plain wooden box. It is just about each other's needs. Dimaryp could help design the latest sky craft and in return have our roof repaired. It is what each of us agree to and accept."

Laeh continued, "Pottery is made of clay, from the Earth, like in your world Lyra. Furniture is made from different materials but the most popular are bamboo, reed and snake grass, we only use wood when trees have fallen. Children begin basket weaving at an early age, it is easy to learn and we always need more baskets. Some of the weavers use that knowledge to apply similar skills to boatbuilding when they are older. We also like to compete with each other to see who can invent an unusual new object, something completely different." Lyra clapped her hands with delight.

"Crystal crafting requires a special technique and is taught by some of the elders," Dimaryp said, joining in, "It is rather a lengthy process, but the results are breath-taking. Large crystals are found in the mountains and smaller ones on riverbeds. Each have different properties, so where some crystals can be heated and moulded like glass, other crystals have to be carefully cut." Lyra sat listening attentively, stroking Doobey who had made himself comfortable on one of the cushions.

"We teach our children the things they need to know, that will keep them strong in mind and body," Laeh explained, "Children are happiest when they are involved in whatever is being done. As they grow and mature, they learn the life skills they need at their own pace. We spend most of our lives amongst Nature and live very long lives, so we can take our time, there is no rush."

* * * * *

Dimaryp wanted to speak about the burden they know children face, living on Earth. As he spoke, Lyra noticed how serious his face became. "Attitudes must change on Earth," he said as he held up his arms, fingers outstretched, and looked painfully into the sky. He lowered his head and brought his hands to his chest and clasping his heart he said, "Attitudes **need** to change on the surface, to bring humanity back to unconditional Love, so we can ALL unite."

"Humans must stop being greedy and selfish," Laeh continued, wagging her finger toward the sky. "They are greedy for anything and everything, some stop at nothing, to get what they want. Imagine someone eating twenty carrots a day for a year because they believe it will give them perfect vision. After that year, they have become unwell and their skin has become carrot coloured. Moderation should be practised in everything. "

Lyra listened eagerly, wanting to hear more. "But why would someone eat twenty carrots a day for a year Laeh?" She was puzzled, and hadn't understood. "Well my child, it was an extreme example. They did something which they should have known would be too much, and it was not until they saw, and felt, what they had done to themselves, that they realised they had gone too far. Greed is an ugly, self-centred trait that helps no-one and needs to be kept in check.

Gratitude on the other hand, is a virtue, it tells the Universe you are ready to receive. And receive good things you will because the Universe is generous, it gives you lots of good things, if you are grateful first. A fine example, is being grateful for waking up each morning and a good time to **begin** being grateful. Then be grateful for having a bed to sleep in, clean clothes to wear, for having a breakfast each morning and also for seeing your family are all well and good." She smiled, already knowing how blessed she was.

* * * * *

Lyra's mind drifted off again. She heard her school friends talking about computer games and networking on their phones. She found it mind blowing and couldn't understand the attraction of screen life when real life was just outside the door. Watching Nature, seeing how it changes through the seasons, fascinated Lyra. What is life behind a screen? She saw how it had taken over her class mates lives, and in the past had tried to interest them in Nature, but failed, disastrously.

"That is one of the reasons you are here my dear," Dimaryp said in answer to Lyra's thoughts. "We know you would like to help your class mates out of the rut they have slipped into. It is stopping them from **really** enjoying their lives." Lyra nodded. "We are showing you ways to help them change how they look at life and we will soon bring other children into yours, to help you." Lyra was very happy to hear this.

"Some of us work with technology, but in areas that will improve lives, not destroy it. We have advanced computers that unite with the trees. At the moment it is mainly for our star ships. We have been monitoring movement on Earth's surface because what happens there, affects the rest of the Universe. I have a great deal more to learn as it is so in-depth, but what I have learnt so far is fascinating," Laeh said.

"Computers that unite with the trees?" Lyra asked in amazement. "Yes Lyra," Dimaryp replied, smiling broadly, "Technology here works with Nature, just like we do." Even the trees are ready to offer assistance, Lyra thought to herself, how awesome that everything seems so kind, helpful and free.

Lyra imagined living in a world like theirs, without the usual rush that happened at home every weekday morning … dad getting ratty if the bathroom wasn't free, mum constantly asking Matty to stop daydreaming into his cornflakes. Herself usually rushing to school after her morning run with Doobey. She could see such a striking difference between their worlds.

"Could I meet with the children I saw earlier?" Lyra suddenly asked. She was curious to see if they were like her. "Yes of course Lyra," Laeh replied and Doobey began scanning the area, as though he had already seen someone, or heard something. Lyra stroked Doobey affectionately, again so happy her faithful friend was there, as usual, sharing such a wonderful adventure.

They stood up and continued walking, leaving the golden structure behind. Ahead of them were wide open fields, very similar to the fields Lyra and Doobey had been playing in, before the Earth had collapsed. Everything in Airumel was so similar to surface Earth, she thought. The trees, bushes and flowers, the birds and animals she had seen, they were all so similar, yet so very different. Lyra wondered again how this difference could have happened.

They walked on for a while passing a group of green wolves, then a yellow bear who seemed to be looking for something. Following Laeh and Dimaryp down a hollow and around some large boulders that had fallen from a mountain some time ago, Lyra noticed a gigantic bell a little way off. She began to hear singing that could only be described as Angels. "Some of the children are practising," Dimaryp told her. She was drawn to what she was hearing and emotion welled up inside of her.

As they passed the huge Golden Bell, Lyra gave it a quick glance, trying to guess for a moment what it could possibly be there for. Beyond the Golden Bell were the children and Doobey let out a little bark. Lyra knew he wanted to play. She stopped him from running to them and leant against a nearby cottage covered in vines, watching intently, intrigued by their voices.

Chapter Seven   The circle of children

The children sang in a language Lyra didn't understand, creating an air of mystery and wonder which sent tingles down the back of her neck. They were standing in a circle, and between each one of them, grew a huge peach flower, similar to a giant daffodil. Lyra saw the smallest child in the centre of the circle take something from a basket to one side of her. She threw it to one of the children in the circle, who caught it, while they continued on with their singing.

As it lay in the child's hand, she looked at it and uttered some words. After a short time the object began to move. Lyra looked at Doobey in amazement, then back to the child's hand. It moved again, and then it changed shape. The child cupped her hands gently over the shape and softly sang a few solo notes. She lifted herself a couple of feet into the air, and opened her hands. Out flew a bird, which spread its multi-coloured wings and flew into the sky.

"Woah!" Lyra exclaimed, "That was amazing!" She looked at the children, then back to Laeh, "Was that magic? How did she do that?" Laeh snapped off a piece of gold that was growing in the middle of a flower, held it in Lyra's direction and said, "Airumel may seem like a magical place Lyra, but if humans trusted in their own inner strength, amazing things would happen in your world too. You must each have Faith in yourselves, Faith that you can really do, **whatever** you desire to do," she said.

Laeh explained that the only way a civilisation can heal itself, is by trusting they can do it. "They can create what they want, how they want, just by having Faith they can do it, the Universe takes care of the rest. We wish to show youngsters like yourself, how to help. Your interest in Nature takes you away from the mind numbing world of technology, and brings you to a world I call, 'Mind Cleansing.'

Fresh minds, young **and** old, will help transform the Earth back into the peaceful, harmonious world it once was, and believe me, it will be done. It is just a matter of each of you, knowing how to use your mind to create a pathway to the Highest Power." Again, Lyra looked surprised, her eyebrows raised as she listened to what she was hearing. "But I still don't understand. **How** do I help?"

"You should be yourself, the best version of yourself. Your strengths will allow others to grow around you. Lead by example, instead of by words, you will see a better result. We can all only do so much, after that, it is up to each individual to choose their own path and how they live it. Laeh looked down for a moment, "Humans have lost their focus. Most do not know how powerful they once were," then she smiled and said, "With courage and determination, **all** will be powerful again."

* * * * *

One of the children in the circle had spotted Lyra and Doobey and was on his way to see who the newcomers were. He was the oldest, Lyra thought, as she watched him come closer. He bowed politely as he reached them and she smiled back. The singing had stopped now and three more children were on their way over. Lyra watched excitedly, as one by one the circle of children came over to greet them.

"My name is Ybur and this one is Lapo," the first boy said, crossing his right arm over his heart area. "Yes and I am Revlis and she is my best friend Latsyrc," a girl wearing a pointy hat said with so much excitement, she looked ready to burst. She politely introduced the children to Lyra, "This is Dlareme, Reppoc, Rebma and Enirtic, the girls," she said, signalling to each one as she spoke, " and Edol, Nori and Leets are the boys," they bowed their heads as their names were called.

Lyra smiled at the children as they gathered around in surprise. Their hands reaching out to touch and greet her and Doobey. She felt a warm friendliness wash over her and was pleased to hear them speak with their mouths. "My name is Lyra and he's my best friend Doobey," she said, playing with Doobey's ears. "We live on the surface, in the world above. We were in the meadows when the Earth collapsed and we fell straight through."

"You come from above!?" Lapo asked excitedly, looking around at the rest of the group who were jumping around, waving their arms in the air. "What is it like?" he said. "We have heard stories about the world above, but we have never been there. Our guardians said it would not be good for us to go there right now." Lyra frowned, "Why, what do you mean?" she asked.

"It would cause us to feel ill because the energy is too low, it is too hostile for children right now," Lapo explained. "Does that mean you could never come and visit me where I live?" Lyra asked curiously. "Not until more humans have learnt to live peacefully," Lapo replied. "When that happens, we will visit and share our friendship."

"We were told some humans are greedy and unkind, which makes many people's lives very difficult," Ybur explained. Lyra wondered why. "Most humans do not give thanks to their Sun for the blessings it shines on them, or to the Earth for the life it brings forth," Latsyrc announced. "Yes and humans do not love the way we do." Revlis joined in. "If we were not truly grateful for everything, **our** lives would become harsh too." Ybur continued. "I think I understand," Lyra replied.

"I live in a house near the meadows with Doobey, my parents and my little brother Matty. I've always lived there, and I like it." She paused, "But I know there are people on Earth who do suffer, badly, some through war, others through lack of food and water, and in those places people have very little. Life becomes too difficult and people die," she said sadly.

She thought about how much she enjoyed her evening meal, but how she usually left the room after eating because mum had turned on the radio and at some point the news came on. Lyra often wondered why they talked so much about things they did little to put right. It made her feel cold and she didn't like that feeling, so, she would take Doobey for a run, or do homework in her bedroom.

Suddenly, as if it had heard, the Great Red Sun appeared in the sky and everywhere became extremely bright. The birds stopped twittering and stood motionless on the branches of the trees. Animals lay quietly amongst the carpet of tiny flowers, and the children stood like statues in a game of Simon says, awaiting Simon's next request. Silence fell upon their world, as they bowed to their Sun and Lyra watched in amazement.

Laeh joined Lyra, who was using her hands to shade her eyes. She explained that this is one of those times when the Sun appears, and everyone stops to give thanks. "We are expressing gratitude for the blessings the Great Sun shines on us, and the beautiful land we live in. We speak words of gratitude for its Light and warmth and the Life and energy it brings." Lyra nodded, deciding she too was very grateful to be there, so she closed her eyes, bowed her head and silently spoke a few words of thanks.

* * * * *

Some minutes had passed when Lyra began to hear rustling, then movement again. Opening her eyes she blinked a few times and looked around. She could no longer see the Sun and life was continuing as before. She looked at Doobey who was running around her, wagging his tail. "I never see humans doing anything like that. Matty and me sometimes sit with mum in the garden, and say thank you to the Earth for all that it gives, but we never talk to the Sun," and she paused.

"Some people visit churches or temples to sing songs and say prayers," she said after a while, "but not to our Sun. They say prayers to their God and believe doing that will save them," and she thought how peculiar that actually sounded. "What do you mean save them, save them from what and where is this God?" Lapo asked.

"They say God is in heaven, way up in the sky and will save humanity from evil by making the world full of Love," she answered. Dimaryp shook his head, "No Lyra, there is only ONE THING that can bring true Love to your world, and that is the people, of course. It has to be the **choice** of the people." Lyra nodded in agreement. The children were clapping their hands and smiling.

"Our Sun is the Light of our world, even when we cannot see it. Your Sun is the Light of your world," Laeh explained. "They are both ancient and mystical, providers of the Light and darkness for the whole of Nature. We give this Majestic Being the respect it deserves. Suns provide warmth, energy, Love and Light to the world it shines on, which helps every living thing to be healthy and grow.

We love Nature. That is why we honour it and work with it. We understand that everything in Nature is a gift, as each one of us are gifts, to each other. You must never forget that Lyra." She agreed with Laeh wholeheartedly, she had always believed that every single life is precious, even the tiny ants that wander around the rocks at the bottom of her garden, looking so aimless. Are actually working tirelessly on their task.

"The song you were singing, what language was that?" She asked the children, "It sounded so beautiful! And what was being held, did it really come to life?" Lyra found that more difficult to understand than a book opening by command. "The language is ancient Airumian, and it was a crystal that came to life, we use them for all sorts of things, there are so many of them," Rebma replied, and giggled, dropping a few as she pulled a large handful out of her pocket to show Lyra.

Ybur picked one up. "This is a lodestone, a very powerful crystal. It can slow down overactive organs in the body, probably due to its magnetic properties. It also helps blood flow through the body with ease," and Ybur placed one in Lyra's hand. "It is far too hard for moulding, but is often used in technology for its ability to store information." Lyra studied the lodestone carefully, she had heard her grandma mention them in the past, but had no idea what they were used for.

"The Golden Bell over there, is used to help us to vibrate higher." Lyra frowned, "Vibrate higher? What do you mean Ybur?" she asked with curiosity. "We are all made of energy, everything, is made of energy, vibrating energy. If your energy is high, you bring high energy back to you. For example, giving Love, Gratitude, Forgiveness, and Joy, all high energy. The Golden Bell can help you to find the high energy that is within you, it is then up to you to use it."

Lyra thought about it then asked, "Can I feel high energy without the Golden Bell?" Laeh was very pleased and impressed with Lyra's question and explained to her that it is possible, but takes practice. "If you desire to succeed, with practice, you will. Imagine it like this Lyra, you are having a bad day, one mishap leads to another and because of this, your mood changes and you snap at someone angrily. You have lowered your energy.

You now have two choices, you can either, continue being angry and attract low energy to you, like anger, sadness, deceit, hurt, fear etc, or, you can stop, take some deep breaths and clear your mind. By clearing your mind, not thinking about it over and over again, things will change and quickly get better. The reason is because you have made a high energy choice to stop feeling angry." Lyra understood this example perfectly.

"Honour your feelings though Lyra," Laeh continued, "If someone annoys you, allow the feeling to be there for a while. Do not feel sad it is there, have no feelings about it, just let it move through you. Allowing it to be there, stops it from having power over you. Do not keep it, or hold onto it, or make stories in your mind about it. You are just being aware it is there, so it can move through you and then it will go." Lyra smiled and nodded, she felt that was something she would like to practise.

* * * * *

"Nori's going to have a session in the Golden Bell, would you like to come Lyra and see what happens?" Ybur asked, helpfully. Lyra blushed shyly, she liked Ybur and wasn't sure why she was being silly. She wanted to go and take a look, but didn't know why she couldn't say yes. She was a little wary of thinking too much in case he heard her. She looked at the Golden Bell, fiddling nervously with Doobey's lead.

Suddenly the children gathered round Lyra again. They were all talking at once, asking questions and overloading her with information. Some were asking what it is really like to live on surface Earth, others were asking if Doobey could talk and what he could do. She focused in on one particular statement though, "Some of the elders are creating stars out there, right now," she heard Lapo say.

Lyra stared at Lapo in astonishment, her mouth fell open as though she was going to gasp. "But, how do, I mean, is it …" Laeh could see that Lyra was visibly shaken with that piece of information. "On a less grand scale though Lyra," she interrupted, "creative energy is first used for focusing the mind." Lyra and the children sat on the grass, she wanted to know more.

"Some of the elders are so advanced they know how to create huge things. Because they are ancient they have been learning for many years," Lapo continued. "Yes, they know how to use their mind to move energy and bring something into existence," Ybur continued, "So even though it seems impossible Lyra, it is possible. I have been trying to create a land craft, but it is different because it is not living." Lyra chuckled, but had another question.

"Do your guardians use the Golden Bell, for things like that, I mean?" she asked. Ybur told Lyra it was rare that any of the guardians used it. "They have spent many years practising the art of creation and object movement. It is not because they are better than us Lyra, they have just been here much longer than us, so they already know of the ancient teachings, and how to use them. We have levels of being and we all learn at our own pace, so there are no misunderstandings."

"Or secrets?" Lyra asked wanting to know more. "What are secrets?" A little voice from the back of the group suddenly asked. They all laughed, it was little Leets the most inquisitive child in the group. "Oh, I'm not sure how you would explain that," Lyra said, feeling lost for words. "A secret is not known by others," Laeh said, seeing that Lyra needed some help, "and something that is supposed to be kept unknown," she went on.

Dimaryp joined in, "In your world Lyra, as you know, people do have secrets. Some are harmless and only used to protect someone's feelings from getting hurt. Other secrets are hurting the whole of humanity, because they are hidden. Life on Earth was changed by secrets that, if known, would set humanity free. Living freely is the key to Joy and Happiness for everyone." Lyra thought about Dimaryp's statement, 'Life on Earth has been changed by hidden secrets.' What did he mean?

"In Airumel we are open with each other and are aware of what each other is thinking," Laeh said, "we would know if one of us was not telling a truth, so there is no use for secrets in Airumel. It would be like carrying a large glass bottle, with a beautiful flower inside and expecting no-one to see it." Lyra nodded excitedly, as she compared the 'flower in the bottle' theory, to thoughts of the mind.

Ybur was aware how curious Lyra was about everything, but also a little shy, "Would you like to be shown the Golden Bell?" Lyra smiled and nodded so Laeh took hold of her hand, "Come child, let me show you about positive energy," and she led Lyra, closely followed by Doobey, into the Golden Bell. As they walked, Lyra noticed again, the feeling of warmth and peace flow over her.

Chapter Eight   Golden Bell Treatment

Inside the Golden Bell it was very warm and rather dark. There was an earthy smell that reminded Lyra of the greenhouses on the park. Laeh placed some crystals on the table which brightened the darkness, then turned to Lyra. "Would you like to have a session yourself Lyra? There is nothing to fear. It will build on your good energy and keep it there for a while," Lyra nodded, she had a faraway look in her eyes.

She was standing, hands on hips, turning, as she viewed this giant bell from the inside. Looking up to the top, the large curved dome appeared to have no clapper, the mechanism that produces the ringing sound. How can a bell make me feel more positive, she thought, and wondered what was going to happen. Without a word, Laeh answered her question once again.

"It is a Resounding Bell Treatment, or RBT." Laeh announced, "The sounds will vibrate deep inside your body and clear away stubborn energy. It is the structure of the bell and the instruments I use, that help with the process. Afterwards you will feel a little lightheaded, then you will notice how simply you see everything, with no opinion," she said reassuringly. "Ooh yes please Laeh. I would love to try it!" She was eager to see how she would feel afterwards.

Laeh directed Lyra to a raised wooden platform and asked her to lie down and make herself comfortable. "Will I need to do anything?" she asked, taking off her jacket, and placing it next to her backpack. "You will need to do nothing Lyra, except relax. That is important, relax and the sounds will flow in and around your mind and body with ease."

Lyra climbed onto the wooden platform and Laeh covered her with a fine mesh cloth. Doobey stood close by, watching intently, ever faithful to his best friend. "Don't worry Doobey," she said, "I'm just getting some RBT." Doobey barked and sat by the platform, ears standing to attention, waiting to see what happened next. He was as curious as Lyra and learnt many things by watching and listening.

Laeh walked over to a long table to choose one of the strange looking instruments on display. Most of them Lyra had never seen before, apart from the Tibetan singing bowls. Auntie Susie had one of those and Lyra had tried to work it once or twice. Laeh told her the treatment was going to be given via the Tibetan bowls, so she chose a medium sized bowl, and a medium sized mallet.

She balanced the bowl in her outstretched hand, knocked it gently with the mallet, and began moving it quickly around the outside edge of the bowl. As she did so, the bowl produced a sound similar to a continuous ringing bell. Laeh knocked the mallet against the bowl again, more sharply this time. The sounds joined instantly, ringing in harmony.

While Lyra relaxed, Laeh picked up the largest bowl. Moving away from the table this time, she knocked the bowl with the mallet. Slowly, a deeper, hollow ringing emerged, connecting to the Golden Bell itself, which sounded like an old church bell. Laeh moved the mallet round and round the outside edge of the bowl, the sound developing into a curious melody as it gathered speed.

The melody darted from one part of the Golden Bell to another, bouncing from left to right as it moved in and out of Lyra's mind and body. A gentle hum could be heard behind the melody and Lyra's body began to tingle. She wriggled as a gentle buzz ran up and down her spine, across her chest, and through her fingers and toes. As the tingling moved around her body, she chuckled every now and again, when the tickle became too much.

After a while Laeh informed Lyra that the session was complete. She replaced the instruments neatly on the table and returned to Lyra who was sitting up looking a little dazed. "How do you feel?" She asked attentively, seating herself next to Lyra. "I do feel slightly lightheaded. I don't know what I was expecting, but I wasn't expecting to feel like this. My mind feels so clear, there are no thoughts at all."

Doobey barked and nuzzled up to Lyra's leg, he was just happy to see Lyra sitting up again. Laeh smiled kindly at Lyra and advised her to stay sitting on the platform for a while. "It will give your mind and body chance to catch up with what just happened," she said, "you have been through a process called regeneration," so she sat listening to the remnant of the echoes as they faded away.

After a while Lyra asked, "Will this help with my maths homework? It takes me the longest time to finish, I often don't remember what to do," and she grinned. "Yes Lyra, it will definitely help, you are now energised and focused, you will understand information you are given much more easily. Pathways in your mind are now clear, ready for new ideas to come through." Lyra wondered how she was going to keep her mind so clear, once she had left Airumel.

"There are many ways Lyra. Food-wise, root vegetables are best because they are still living. Pulses and seaweeds are also full of the minerals your body needs to stay healthy and strong. If you have an allergy it will affect you, research which food will heal it. Adding sugar and salt to your food will not help the body, it is bad for everyone. The music you listen to, in fact anything you listen to, if it makes you feel Joyful, it will leave you feeling Joyful, and that is the key."

Lyra wondered if there were other ways she could keep herself feeling positive. "Be around people that help you feel at peace, people who make you smile, people who leave you with a warm glow," Laeh advised. "Also it is best not to think about the past or the future, unless it makes you happy. The past holds guilt and blame, the future can make you worry.

Never worry Lyra, just take things day by day. Start by sitting quietly, listening to yourself breathing deeply. Maybe learn how to practise Yoga. Buy a book, or borrow one from the library and learn to do the exercises that suit you. Keep going out in Nature every day, and stay around trees, they are **very** spiritual. Bury your bare feet in the Earth as often as you can to ground yourself. You are literally planting yourself like a tree, and drink plenty of clean, fresh water from wells that are supplied by mountain springs, that is a real treat for your body."

Lyra smiled, remembering the Spring Well in her own back garden. "Yes Lyra, we put it there, but it became hidden when people who lived there before your family, closed it off and covered it with soil. We made many outlets across Earth, they are supplied from the mountains." Lyra felt a little overwhelmed. "Wow, okay," and wondered how they could have done that. "It has been there for many of your years, way before the time your house was built," Laeh answered.

It had become clear to Lyra that these beings were very advanced. How had this happened? Where had they come from? The book in the Green Sanctuary said they arrived here during some kind of war. Was the war on the surface of Earth? Did they develop their creative power to such an advanced level during that time, or did they already have it? ... How long had they been watching her?

"We have been with you all of your life Lyra, we knew babies would be born that would grow up to help your world. We watch over them as they grow, it is easy when you are invisible. At a certain point, we introduce ourselves." Lyra smiled nervously, as she pondered over times in her life when she could have been watched. I may not have been alone? She shrugged it off, smiled and switched her thoughts.

She remembered a conversation mum and Auntie Susie had become engrossed in. It was regarding the Earth, and how great your body feels when you bury your feet in the ground, and they had all done it that day, while sitting in the garden. Laeh was impressed with how Lyra had turned her thoughts from something that began to worry her, into something that made her feel grounded. "That is good Lyra and it will keep you feeling positive, even if the day is not," she said.

"Just like a trampled flower, feelings can get trampled on too. A plant is already grounded in the Earth, unless it is destroyed, it will grow again." Laeh explained. "Being in Nature in the sunshine, will automatically ground you, especially around trees, they are the great Grandfathers of Wisdom and hold powerfully high energy. You can ground yourself just by being around these Earth Angels."

* * * * *

Doobey got up and trotted over to the doorway of the Golden Bell, he looked at Lyra, then Laeh, and wandered outside. "I think Doobey is getting a little warm in here, **his** coat will not come off," Laeh said winking at Lyra. She agreed, and they both laughed. She felt okay now, the floaty feeling seemed to have gone, so they decided to leave the Golden Bell. She jumped off the platform and went to get her things while Laeh made her way to the opening.

As they left the Golden Bell they were met by Ybur and Nori. "Have you finished now Laeh?" Ybur asked politely, "I am going to give Nori a treatment," he explained, watching Nori as he juggled five crystals with ease. "Yes, that will be good," Laeh answered, "Thank you both for being patient," and she went over to join Dimaryp, who was relaxing on the grass.

"How do you feel Lyra?" Ybur asked politely, "Has it helped?" Lyra smiled, she definitely felt more alert and free from tiring thoughts. She sometimes worried about people who try to overpower her. "My mind seems so clear and free, crystal clear," she said. Ybur smiled, "That is good. It means it worked. I trust my treatment will work on Nori too," and they disappeared inside the Golden Bell.

Lyra blushed, then noticed the other children were playing with Doobey, so she went over to join them. "How do you feel after the Big Bell?" Revlis asked. "I feel super charged and ready for anything," Lyra announced, and thought about what she had done so far. She knew now why she had felt elated this morning. She wondered what other surprises were going to be revealed to her.

She looked over at Laeh and Dimaryp. "How is it they look so young when they must be over five hundred years old? Humans usually die around the age of eighty or ninety and they don't look like that. They look old, with wrinkles and droopy skin. Some live to be a hundred, but not very many."

The children started chattering between themselves and one or two of them made rather strange noises. "How old are your guardians Lyra," Latsyrc asked with curiosity. "I think my mum's thirty six and my dad is forty. I know that because we had a big party for him earlier this year," Lyra replied. "They are very young," Latsyrc said, "We play around for years and years before we have children."

"They look like that because they can recreate themselves however they want, so can we," Lapo informed Lyra. "Really? How do you do that?" Lyra asked, not knowing what to expect. "We decide we want to look different .... And, we change ourselves. There is nothing, '**secret**', about it," he said. They all laughed, then Lyra stopped, she was confused.

"So, if you decide you want to look different, you can just change yourselves?" she asked, eager to know more. "Yes, we imagine how we wish to appear, we go into a type of trance while we connect with our creative energy, and then we become what we imagine. We could do it every day if we wanted to."

Lyra stared at them for a moment in disbelief, she was also a little bothered at how confusing that would be, changing their appearance whenever they wanted to. "It is not as confusing as you imagine," she heard Laeh say, "We see and know each other by our spirit, so we know who each one of us are at all times, even when we are out of our vessel." Lyra grinned but felt humbled by them.

She wanted to know more about vibrations and asked, "So tell me, have I got this right, being in a high vibration brings you good things, and being in a low vibration brings bad things?" Dimaryp came over, "Yes, that is very good my dear, it shows you are beginning to understand. Your thoughts, words and actions, affect the way other people think, speak and behave towards you. The greatest thing about high vibration is, no-one can take it away from you. The only one capable of doing that, is yourself."

This concerned Lyra a little. "So if I lose my high vibration ..." she stopped as Dimaryp shook his head. "It is more a case of allowing it to lower. "This is why you have to be mindful of what you say and do, but **especially** of what you think. In your world, thinking can be done without anyone knowing. Outwardly it seems to have gone unnoticed, but the Universe notices **everything**. Lyra listened intently, knowing she was learning something powerful.

Laeh joined them. "Maybe this is easier to understand Lyra. We give and receive higher energy when we are being positive. We keep higher energy by staying positive. We lower our energy when we are negative. Never be sad Lyra, that is lower energy too, you can raise your energy again at any moment just by choosing to be in a positive mind." Lyra smiled, this made a lot of sense to her.

She looked around at the children and noticed how full of Joy they all were, a little like Doobey before going for a run. "How old are you all?" Lyra asked, thinking maybe the children were also older than they looked, they seemed older. "We do not know exactly Lyra," Revlis explained, "None of us do. We see **every** day as a celebration of life, not just the day we were born." Lyra understood that, but thought it a little strange they didn't even know how old they were.

"We only think about the moment we are living in Lyra," came a voice from around the corner of the cottage. The boy appeared, and joined the rest of the group. He looked a little different to the other children, he wasn't as slender as they were. Lyra thought he looked like one of the boys at her school. "If we think about times gone by, it takes us back, and because we strive to go forward, it makes no sense thinking back," the boy said.

"Yes we see every moment as a new beginning. We are trying to better ourselves all the while and the best way to do that, is to see every moment as new." Revlis explained. "Our guardians go back from time to time, if there is a need to, but they know how to come forward with a clear mind," she said.

"That is Dlog," Latsyrc announced with delight, "He is our special child," she went on, realising he hadn't been introduced, and Dlog bowed his head. "He has a special gift that only a few of us have." Lyra was fascinated, "What kind of special gift?" She asked. The children looked at each other and then they looked at Dlog. "I can talk to our Great Sun," he said very seriously. "How do you do **that**?" Lyra asked, picturing Dlog standing somewhere high up.

"You have a good imagination Lyra," Dlog observed. "I do usually go to a mountainside and find a comfortable spot, then I sit and I meditate. In my calm, clear headspace I am ready to connect with the Great Sun, and I wait until it comes. The Great Sun is ancient and wise. It speaks to my mind and tells me of things that are personal to me, and of things others should know. I do not know how I do this, it happened one day while meditating," Dlog said modestly.

"How wonderful, that must be awesome! What kind of things does the Great Sun tell you?" Lyra wanted to know. Dlog spoke of a time when they were in need of a certain crystal and the Great Sun had taken him, in his mind, to a place no-one had ever seen. On discovering the unknown place, he found it packed full of the crystals they had been searching for, to use in building their latest sky craft.

As Lyra imagined The Great Sun talking with Dlog, and helping him find the hidden place, she remembered The Oracle and the challenge she had accepted earlier in the day. "I've been challenged to find The Oracle," she told the children. "Laeh and Dimaryp said if I can find her, she will assist me in discovering things about myself that will help me."

"But not yet?" Latsyrc enquired. "I don't know how long I have here, so it will be soon." Lyra answered slowly. "We were just getting to know you," Dlareme said. They were noticeably disappointed, but in Lyra's mind she would return if she was able to. "The Oracle will show you fascinating things," Dlog told Lyra. She smiled and turned to Laeh. She didn't want to miss meeting The Oracle and Laeh knew that, "Whenever you are ready my child, and I do believe you will find her," Laeh assured her.

Everyone knew The Oracle, she sometimes came with artwork and clay wares for barter. She was a respected elder and one of the highly enlightened. The children had a special connection with The Oracle and visited her often. They loved how interesting she made everything, and they learnt many different things from her.

The Oracle set games and quizzes for the children to solve, based around different topics. The children loved these games, they had so much fun while they were learning. Sometimes they played in the high branches of the treehouse. It was a huge broad tree with long, wide branches, giving lots of places to hide.

The Oracle showed them how to make musical instruments and then taught them how to play. As music was an important part of all their lives, it was interesting to know how the instruments were created. They made flutes and different types of drums out of bamboo, some went on to create xylophones when they were older. They loved playing around with music, producing beautiful songs for different occasions and often used them during relaxation times.

Revlis and Latsyrc began nudging each other and giggling, "Can we come with you Lyra, we could help you find The Oracle?" Latsyrc suddenly asked. "You already know where The Oracle lives Latsyrc. This is Lyra's challenge, and it is her task," Laeh explained. The children liked Lyra, and of course Doobey, and didn't feel ready to see them go, but they also knew it was useless complaining. She was here for a purpose and they couldn't get in her way.

* * * * *

Lyra said goodbye to the children, although they weren't quite sure what she meant. 'Goodbye' was a word they never used. "If you say, until we meet again, they will understand you better," Dimaryp suggested. Lyra turned to the children and told them how wonderful it had been meeting them, and she 'trusted' she would see them all again soon. Laeh and Dimaryp nodded and smiled, they knew Lyra would return soon.

The children gathered around Lyra, touching her gently. Revlis and Latsyrc kissed her hands as Lyra felt their warmth and friendliness again. Doobey jumped up onto his back legs, his tongue hanging out, and barked a few times, just to let them know he had also enjoyed their company. The children giggled, rubbing Doobey's neck and stroking him as Lyra watched, preparing herself for the challenge and feeling very determined.

Just before they set off, Ybur came out of the Golden Bell followed by Nori, who was looking very bright, "Are you leaving Lyra?" Ybur enquired. "Yes, I'm going to find The Oracle," she said, pleased to see him again. "I trust we will see you both soon?" he asked. Lyra smiled, "I believe we will return as soon as we can," she answered politely. Ybur crossed his right arm over his heart and bowed his head once more.

Chapter Nine   Lyra's challenge begins

Lyra and Doobey started walking as Laeh and Dimaryp moved on ahead, leading the way for a while. Doobey ran over to a nearby crystal river. He trotted through the water, stopping for a moment to gaze at its beauty, then turned to see where Lyra was. The three of them had stopped.

"I've no idea which way to go Laeh, could you give me a clue?" she asked. "No Lyra, but it is fine if anything wishes to help you along the way," Laeh replied. We are only a thought away. Trust your intuition, The Oracle is not that far."

Lyra looked over at Doobey who was busily drinking from the river. "You did say the water is safe to drink, didn't you?" Lyra enquired, remembering it wasn't water as she knew it. "Yes Lyra, it is fine, it will do you both good, it is spring water, but with many additional minerals. Nothing here will harm either of you, my child." Laeh said kindly, and waited to see which direction Lyra was going to choose.

"My intuition is telling me to go that way," she said, pointing to the east. She smiled at Laeh and Dimaryp, "I'm so happy I met you all and discovered so many new things. Will I see you again soon?" she questioned, "Keep your energy high Lyra. We **will** meet again, it is definitely meant to be," Laeh answered. They hugged each other, then waved, as Lyra and Doobey set off.

* * * * *

It was a beautiful day, the Great Sun was shining brightly, somewhere, although Lyra wasn't sure where and giggled as she remembered how the Great Sun loves to play. She stroked Doobey's ear as they walked, concentrating on how to find The Oracle. The land was wide and open and groups of trees could be seen everywhere. Lyra believed with her heart that she would find her.

They passed some effarigs who appeared to be having some kind of a game. Each in turn, were skipping towards a tree, jumping to touch the tallest branches and then skipping back again. Lyra chuckled as she watched Doobey join in. He bounced onto a clump of grass, using it as a type of spring board to gain height, failing miserably. He tried a few times, but lost interest when he realised it just wasn't possible.

They continued walking and looking for large trees. After a while Lyra stopped, she took a deep breath in and let it slowly out. She put her hands above her eyes and surveyed the land. "I have a feeling we should keep going that way," she said, pointing again towards the East, "I'm hungry though, let's stop for a while," she said, taking off her backpack and dumping it on the ground.

Doobey poked his nose into it. "Nose out Doobey!" she ordered as she reached inside for his biscuits. She threw him a couple into the air, which he had no trouble catching in his mouth, then she opened the bottle of water and took a long drink. She sat down and helped herself to another sandwich as she pondered over what The Oracle would tell her.

"So Doobey, we're going to find The Oracle," she said, giving him some more of his biscuits. Doobey wagged his tail as he finished eating. Lyra looked around and spotted a group of beings in the distance who she hadn't seen. They didn't seem to have noticed Lyra and Doobey as they were sitting in a circle and appeared to be meditating. Closer, was a noil quietly playing with flutterbies, it looked like a big green pussy cat.

Lyra reflected on her day so far. When I woke up this morning, I knew there was something different about the day, but I would never have imagined that Lyra Barnes, of Fairbank Lane, Beaconsfield, would be inside the Earth, under a bright red Sun, near a friendly green lion, after meeting special beings, on her way to find The Oracle? She caught herself … deep in thought, eyebrows raised and began to laugh.

The noil wandered over. He sniffed at Doobey and Doobey yapped at him until he stopped. The noil then put one of his large furry paws on Doobey's paw and gave him a long stare. It wasn't an aggressive stare, just a curious one, as though he had many things to say to Doobey, but didn't know where to begin. Doobey yapped at the noil again. "Would you like a sandwich," Lyra asked the noil, but the noil wasn't interested. "Are you looking for someone Mr Noil?" she giggled, "Because we are."

The noil turned his head and gazed at Lyra for a moment, then, yawning and stretching, he lay flat on the tangerine grass. Lyra was glad he was a friendly noil. It was difficult to believe, this creature was so gentle compared to what she had been told about the lions who live on Earth. "We're going to find The Oracle, but we don't know where she lives. I don't suppose you're here to give me a clue?" Lyra asked the noil. Again the noil yawned lazily, blowing off one of the flutterbies that had landed on his paw, as he exhaled.

Doobey jumped up and began barking at the noil, lowering his chin to the Earth and growling, almost as though he was telling him off. He placed his front paws in readiness and bared his teeth. The noil ignored Doobey's angry challenge, making a sound like a loud contented purr, then resting his head across his paws, he closed his eyes and went to sleep.

"What's wrong with you Doobey, why so angry?" Lyra asked, unsure of what had just happened. To Lyra's amazement a voice replied, "Noil is being ignorant to you." She almost jumped out of her skin, "What!! Did you just speak?" He looked coyly at Lyra, head to one side and said, "Yes it was me, Doobey the dog," then barked and rubbed his nose on Lyra's leg. Lyra stared at Doobey in disbelief, then laughed as she ruffled the fur around his neck playfully.

How did **that** happen, she wondered, and how awesome! It must be the spirit of Airumel she thought. She shared her last sandwich with Doobey, then decided the noil wasn't there to help. "Come Doobey let's carry on, it can't be that much further. I can ask for Laeh if we can't …. Oops! Stop, I must imagine a good outcome to this challenge, I must imagine us finding The Oracle," she told Doobey.

After recovering from the surprise of hearing her dog talk, they chatted excitedly about their adventures, speaking of things they had wanted to tell each other for quite some time. Lyra was amazed this was happening, they could communicate with each other, properly now. She realised it was more believable because it had happened in Airumel, amid so many other unusual things.

After walking for a while, they reached the big hill and Doobey ran on ahead to investigate, looking eagerly about. Again he saw groups of trees scattered around, some quite large, but none contained a treehouse. He turned to Lyra as she caught up with him and told her the treehouse was nowhere to be seen.

Lyra scanned the area carefully, studying each tree as she saw it while Doobey stood on his hind legs, still looking around. Suddenly a plant in the distance began moving unusually. "A big red plant over there, I think it's waving to us," Doobey said helpfully. Lyra looked, but could not see where. "Between the two small trees," he said. Lyra focused on the area where Doobey was gazing, then spotted it. "I can see it Doobey and wow, it really is big!" she shouted excitedly, "Come on, let's see what it wants!"

They began sprinting across the tangerine grass, until they came to a patch of shrubs. They tiptoed carefully through them, being cautious not to trample any down. They splashed through a deep stream, where Lyra soaked her trainers, then continued on until they reached the two small trees. There between them, was the reddest plant Lyra had ever seen.

She stopped and looked at the plant, it was **most** unusual. It grew from what looked like a very large bulb. The plant was tall, solid and red, with unusual looking flowers and leaves. At the centre of the opened flower was a diamond shaped dish, similar to an ornate stand, golden in colour with fancy twirls at each of the four corners. The pointy lilac leaves that grew out of the thick red stem, were edged with a scarlet border.

She walked slowly towards the plant, not knowing what to expect. "Come closer Lyra, I have something to share with you," came a voice from the plant. Lyra stopped and gasped in disbelief. She walked closer and stood in front of it. "You are seeking something, is that correct?" the plant asked. "Yes red plant, we are on our way to find The Oracle, who lives in a large treehouse," she said, feeling a little like Dorothy, in The Wizard of Oz.

She leant over the plant and inhaled its sweet scent. "I am The Sun Goddess plant but please call me SG for short," the plant said with a polite, female tone. Lyra giggled then nodded, still looking with curiosity at the plant. "Let me help you find what you are searching for Lyra," the plant suggested … "It is not just your eyes that you see with. Seek with Your Whole Being." SG rustled its leaves, then stood quietly and waited.

Lyra didn't know what SG had meant, but decided SG wasn't going to say any more. She walked towards a large group of nearby trees, puzzling over it as she walked. She glanced at each of the trees and decided, "These trees are way too small, The Oracle must be somewhere else." Seek with Your Whole Being … what on Earth did SG mean? She made her way back.

"Let me explain. You must use your senses Lyra," SG advised. "My senses?" Lyra asked inquisitively. "Yes Lyra, not just sight. You have other senses, touching, hearing, tasting, and smelling, focus on your goal, to find The Oracle." Lyra realised there was more to finding The Oracle than just looking for her. Laeh had believed she could do it, so she knew it could be done.

She stood for a while, hand under her chin, thinking, then glanced at Doobey and said, "I have an idea, let's stand over there where we can feel the breeze, maybe that will help," and she started to walk. Doobey trotted alongside Lyra, through the undergrowth and out into a clearing. She stopped, opened her jacket, and stood like a scarecrow, arms outstretched, head held high and waited.

A few minutes passed by and the sound of the leaves rustled in the trees, almost like they were calling to her, but nothing happened. Lyra waited, then she began twirling around, but stopped when she became dizzy. She steadied herself and waited. She felt the breeze blow across her face as she took a deep breathe. Again the trees rustled in the wind, but still nothing happened. Doobey stood next to Lyra, patiently waiting as he watched two birds dance with each other, as they flew across the sky.

I must only think of one thing, she told herself, as she waited, and that is to find the treehouse and The Oracle. To keep focused, she created a little song, "Our challenge, find The Oracle, we will find The Oracle," she sang, repeating it over and over again, getting faster and more determined each time, allowing no other thought to take over that one thought. Without realising, Lyra was making a connection to The Oracle's energy.

 After a while Lyra stopped. First there was silence, then … the distinct sound of a drum, filtering through to her ears. It was slow and hypnotic, pulsating a rhythmic beat that seemed to be calling back to them. "Doobey, can you hear that? Maybe it's The Oracle!" she shouted excitedly. Standing for a moment and listening, she was wondering where the drumbeats were coming from.

She ran over to SG, "I think I must go now, it really was nice to meet you SG," she said politely, wanting to show her gratitude, "I must say I have never met a plant like you before, you are very special, thank you for helping us." The Sun Goddess plant rustled its leaves again and said, "May the Universe be with you Lyra."

They started walking, listening for the drumbeats getting louder, when Doobey noticed a faint smell of cooking wafting through the air. He lifted his nose and sniffed loudly. "I smell food," Doobey said, licking his lips and drooling. Lyra stopped and took in a deep breath. "You're right Doobey, so can I, but who would be cooking? Are we imagining it?" SG reminded them, "Let your senses guide you."

They walked on towards the smell of the food, sniffing the air as they went. Lyra knew they were heading in the right direction because the drumbeats were becoming more noticeable. The beats began to gather speed, getting louder, they started to run, meandering their way through trees and bushes.

The wonderful aroma was now filling the air the closer they came to the sound of the drumbeats. They continued running until suddenly …. "There!!" Lyra shouted, pointing to the biggest tree she had ever seen in her life. The drumming ceased and Lyra stopped in her tracks as The Oracle appeared on the high balcony of the treehouse.

She held out her arms to greet them, smiling down at them kindly. Lyra stared in amazement, not knowing what to say or what to do. "I give Honour to your Soul. Come closer my friends," she said, bowing her head and crossing her right arm over her heart, "Let me see you both." Lyra moved closer, looked up at her and asked in a rather timid voice, "Are you The Oracle?"

The Oracle continued smiling and said, "I am Anez, or better still Annie, but yes I am also known as The Oracle. You are Lyra and you are Doobey," she stated knowingly, as she looked at them in turn, "Is that not so?" Lyra nodded, happy her challenge was complete. "Yes we are Annie, and Dimaryp said if we could find you, you would tell me things about myself," unsure if she needed to explain.

The Oracle, still smiling replied, "My child, there is plenty for that. Would you like to freshen up and are you hungry, would you like to eat something? Doobey, what about you?" Lyra looked at her hands and frowned, "Yes please Annie, I think these need washing."

"Then you must come to Annie. Are you ready?" The Oracle lowered her arms and quickly raised them again. Lyra and Doobey looked at each other, but before they had time to think, they found themselves lifting into the air, floating towards the treehouse and settling on the balcony next to The Oracle. "Oh my goodness, nothing surprises me now!" Lyra screamed with delight, "I should have guessed something like that was going to happen!"

* * * * *

After she had freshened up and Doobey had finished off a large bowl of soup, they sat down on the balcony and began to talk. Lyra was curious why The Oracle had cooked. She thought the people of Airumel didn't eat, "Do **you** eat food Annie?" The Oracle laughed, "No Lyra, but you two do."

She told Lyra that cooking was a hobby she enjoyed doing, occasionally. "Sometimes friends come over and eat, they say it can be comforting, I find it relaxing to cook," she said, "We do not need food to sustain us, like in your world, we have the Great Sun for that, but I love cooking from Nature, there is so much delight to be found everywhere."

Lyra smiled at The Oracle, she already liked her. She had an Aura similar to her mother's. Doobey glanced at Lyra and then at The Oracle, he felt it was going to get boring for a while, so he sprawled himself out across the balcony, closed his eyes and went to sleep.

The Oracle sat back against the thick blue trunk of the tree and studied Lyra. After a while she said, "There is something we call Harmony Lyra," she stopped again for a moment, still observing Lyra closely, "Most of your people, they do not understand how powerful it is. Harmony will remove barriers and bring Unity where there is none. Do you understand Harmony Lyra?" She wasn't sure what The Oracle meant. She thought it was about feeling good, so she asked, "Do you mean like how it is here?"

Chapter Ten   Wisdom is Given

The Oracle wished Lyra to understand just how powerful Harmony is, "Yes Lyra, life in Airumel is the outcome of living in Harmony." She smiled at her, then took in a very deep breath. She lifted her arms as she inhaled, then lowered them as she breathed slowly out.

"I would like to take you on a journey Lyra, you could call it a journey of self-discovery. It is a journey you make in your mind. The things you have seen here are very different to your world and you are feeling overwhelmed. I can take you to meet your Higher Self, the self within you, who sees and knows you, and knows the Wisdom you all once had. Would you like to understand more clearly?" Lyra didn't need to think, "Yes please Annie," she gushed. "That would be awesome!"

The Oracle went to the doorway of the treehouse and picked up a drum. The top of the drum was wider than the bottom, and it had a piece of thick material stretched tightly across it. "We use this special material, it is similar to the animal skin used for drum tops in your world." she explained. Lyra nodded and watched intently as The Oracle made herself comfortable on the rug.

Observing Lyra's curiosity, The Oracle wanted to share some Wisdom, "Lyra, we can all find Inner Peace, even in the midst of chaos. Life is meant to be challenging, it is what helps us to grow positively. By staying calm and making our highest choice, during challenging times, we become stronger. This helps us to find Inner Peace because we are showing everything unconditional Love, the Love that asks for nothing in return." Lyra listened with great interest.

The Oracle explained to Lyra that Inner Peace is found in the now, any now. "In the now?" Lyra asked. "The moment you are living in, is always 'right now.' Anxiety is the opposite of Peace and comes from worries about the past and doubts about the future. The higher our thoughts are, the grander our feelings will be. It is then that we are connecting to the Most High. Inner Peace comes from being in the 'now' with the Most High." Lyra nodded.

"Make yourself comfortable Lyra and relax. Listen to the sound of the drum while you focus on breathing deeply. I will start with a slow beat." Lyra kicked off her damp trainers and shuffled herself into a cross-legged position on the rug. The Oracle began tapping a slow rhythm as Lyra sat listening, very still and content. She began taking deep breaths in, and out, in, and out. It was very calming and Lyra somehow found it easy to focus only on her breathing, while the drumming continued.

She had become immersed in the drumbeats when The Oracle said, "Lyra, I would like you to put one positive thought in your mind. It can be about anything you wish, but it has to be something that makes you feel very happy," Lyra smiled, that's easy she thought, it's Doobey of course! "With that thought, allow it to blossom into a beautiful picture and in that picture, you are there with the Joyful thought." Lyra continued smiling as she remembered again, the day she first saw Doobey.

Matty was only a few months old at the time and mum was often busy looking after the new baby. Dad had noticed how lonely Lyra appeared to be sometimes and between them they had secretly made the decision to buy Lyra a puppy. Mum and Lyra had just finished eating supper one evening when dad's car pulled up outside.

They had been talking about how life was a little different now, because of the baby. Lyra remembered seeing dad walk into the room holding a little bundle in a blanket, she had looked at mum, who had shrugged. It was then that Lyra had jumped out of the chair to see what it was, knowing it was for her, and to her delight, found the sweetest, cutest puppy. She was overjoyed.

Lyra giggled as she remembered that first night, when she didn't want to go to bed. She wanted to stay with the best present she'd ever had. Mum wouldn't let the pup sleep in the bedroom, but had convinced Lyra to leave her new friend and go to bed, by saying they would go into town the next day, to buy some things for him. Lyra giggled again as she remembered the funny, squeaky toys they had bought and the wicker basket, with the soft, fluffy blanket for the puppy to sleep on.

Lyra was now in a very happy place. Slowly and quietly The Oracle spoke again, "Lyra, you are now feeling Joy, focus on that feeling and keep that feeling inside of you. The happiness you were focusing on has put you in a state of Joy. Only when you are in a state of Joy, can you make great things happen."

Chapter Eleven Journey to Higher Self

Lyra seemed to be floating along with great purpose. Nothing or no-one could stop her from feeling that way. She began seeing pictures flash before her closed eyes. Pictures of when she was younger, during different stages of her life, and feeling the emotion as each picture was revealed. She saw pictures of how different her life had become with Doobey, and how together, they'd had so many adventures in Nature.

After a while the pictures became more recent. A picture of her leg in plaster and the feeling of dismay on realising she would be more housebound until it had healed. There were pictures of dad's fortieth birthday party and the large gathering of people that had been there. Another was of Lyra, trying to get away from the noise and commotion of that day, escaping into the garden with Doobey.

Lyra then saw pictures of her waking up this morning, and a close up of her face after seeing the Sun shining through the curtains, realising it was a great day for exploring. Pictures of the sheer Joy she was feeling from being in Nature. Lyra already knew of her connection to Nature, but it was more than that. She realised Nature was deeply ingrained in her and that since a small child, Nature had played a large part in her life.

The Oracle slowed the drumming and began speaking. "Lyra, we have to go deeper, we have only scratched the surface, are you ready to learn more about yourself?" Lyra nodded in The Oracle's direction, she was still focusing hard, but keen to answer. "That is excellent," and while slowly tapping the drum, The Oracle took in a deep breath, let it slowly out and continued.

"There is a truth about trees I wish you to know. ALL trees are connected. If you could see below the Earth you would know. The roots of every tree, join with every other tree, to form a network of communication. Trees talk to each other under the Earth via their roots." Lyra gasped in surprise.

"The whole of Nature is the same, it is connected. We are ALL connected. The reason for this is simple, it is so we are aware when each of us is going through difficult times in our lives, as well as the joyful times. It is to understand others and give support if needed, without taking the power of helping themselves away. Humans are very powerful. You, are very powerful Lyra, and being able to read Auras, gives you a wonderful advantage." Lyra listened intently.

The Oracle leant into the drum, now playing a different rhythm. The beats became a little faster, creating an air of expectation. "I will guide you to your Higher Self," she said. Lyra continued to listen, eyes tightly shut. The Oracle beat the drum, and it quickly gathered speed. She pounded the drum, louder now and faster, looking out into the distance, then up into the branches of the tree. Her head fell against her chest as though her neck had turned to jelly, and as she raised it, she called out to the Source, the Most High, for assistance.

The Oracle swayed from side to side in a trance-like state as she beat the drum, hypnotised by the sounds she was playing. Lyra breathed deeply, feeling great Joy as she pictured Doobey and the wonderful adventures they had already had. The Oracle played on, swaying with the drumbeats as she turned them into a different rhythm, then with one last beat of the drum, The Oracle stopped.

A quiet calm fell across the treehouse … An echo broke the silence a little way off … another was heard further away … then a third, way in the distance, before the calm peacefulness returned. In that stillness, Lyra's mind had been taken away from all past and future thoughts, she was now in a deep meditation. Lyra was feeling bliss.

She seemed to be drifting along in a bubble, high in the sky. She could see a thick blue mist ahead of her. The bubble drifted on with Lyra tucked safely inside. It drifted through the mist, until Lyra could see a figure a little way off. As she came closer, she noticed the figure looked very much like an older version of herself. Lyra's heart began beating fast.

The vision Lyra was seeing opened out into a clear, wide space and she saw them sitting on what looked like a large bale of hay. She felt incredible Joy as she met with her Higher Self. They hugged tightly, sharing moments of completeness, before Lyra's Higher Self backed away, still holding Lyra's hands and said, "Well, here you are my curious younger self, what would you like to know?"

Lyra was so full of questions, she didn't know where to start. She stared at her Higher Self for a while, then asked, "Where have you been until now?" Higher Self explained that she has always been with her, "I will continue to be with you until we are no longer apart. You are not able to feel me when you are not asking or not looking inside. In moments like these we will connect because, you are asking and you are looking inside … you are full of Joy."

"What do you mean by 'no longer apart' are we not one already, if you are part of me?" Higher Self smiled, "Of course, for sure we are one already. The key is to know how to connect to me, and then how to stay connected." She explained to Lyra that being at Peace with the moment, every moment, will keep her connected to Higher Self.

Lyra wanted to know more, "So even if I can't see you, you are still with me?" There had been times when Lyra could have seriously injured herself while playing carelessly, but had been protected. Lyra felt like there was a higher power helping her and had read about Guardian Angels. "Yes I am always with you. I am here to help. I will offer signs to guide you, if you ask. You will notice these signs, if you look and listen." Lyra pondered on this for a while.

"If you're offering signs to guide me, what are these signs?" Higher Self explained that the signs are so obvious they are usually ignored. "Signs appear where you look, humans believe it just happened like that, for no reason. Do not doubt your intuition, it is also your Higher Self speaking to you. I will answer you if you ask a question. The answer will appear anywhere, this is why you have to look and listen," came the wise reply.

"You should get used to meditating, sitting quietly by yourself and breathing deeply. When doing so, you tune in to your Higher Self, like tuning into a radio station. When you are meditating regularly, you will notice how calm you become, where nothing really bothers you. In those times we come together on a higher level of understanding. Eventually you will feel like this all the time, it is then we become one, forever."

Lyra was fascinated. She sat for a while smiling at her Higher Self. "How, I mean what actually happens? Will we be like an Angel?" Higher Self smiled with affection, suddenly appearing very much like Lyra's mum. "Yes that is good. It is a process your heart and mind go through. When we are on the same wavelength, I am able to show you wisdom **all** the time and keep you safe, **all** the time. You will find it difficult to be around people who make you feel uncomfortable and easy to be with people who make you feel happy and at ease."

Lyra wanted to know more. "Are you able to see my future?" She asked. "That is a difficult question to answer without confusing you, but I will speak as simply as possible. I am aware of the choices you have in your future. I can see pathways of opportunity for you, stretching out in all directions.

Whatever choice you make at each pathway, will affect your future. So you see, it would be difficult to know your exact future, without knowing which choices you make. I will help with your choices, but only if you ask and listen. It is up to you if you follow my advice."

Lyra was now captivated with what she was hearing. "So, if I did listen to all your advice, what **could** you see me doing in the future?" Higher Self smiled, she was aware how determined this younger, less knowledgeable version of herself could be. "If you stay on the path of growth and follow everything I advise, I see you working as an Educator in primary schools, teaching children about the power of trees. How to plant, grow and care for different species and maybe taking children out on field trips, to really involve them in Nature." Lyra smiled happily.

"Remember though Lyra, do not feel sad or disappointed if you make a choice that you later realise was not such a good one for you. In those times you take yourself back a step or two, but do not linger there and do not worry, there is always something to be learnt in those times. See the lesson, and learn from it." She held Lyra's hands tightly and looked deep into her eyes.

"Lyra, I am just a question away. I will help you with signs that you will see or hear. It could be a song on the radio, or words that suddenly appear in your head and will not go away. You could see something as you walk that jogs your memory, or notice a particular time repeating itself on different clocks, read about them and see what they mean. You might see a picture on the side of a van or a phrase while reading a book. Remember, they come at the right time. They are pointers and reminders. Look and listen Lyra, look and listen!"

The image of Lyra's Higher Self started to fade and her voice became faint as the sound of the drum beats filtered back through to Lyra. It drew Lyra back to the treehouse and onto the rug where she was sitting. Without moving an inch, The Oracle had taken Lyra on a journey she would never forget, but she was unable to open her eyes. Lyra heard the sound of a little cry, then a feeling of hurt welled up inside of her. It felt like a huge lump in her throat.

A small timid voice entered Lyra's mind which said, "You blamed me ... you blamed me for things I don't understand. You sat on the bed and said," You're not important anymore, I don't like you," after seeing baby Matty with mum. "Why don't you like me? I feel hurt and lost. You trod on a rusty nail and called me an idiot. Why did you call me an idiot? I didn't do it on purpose, it was hurting and bleeding. There have been so many times I felt alone. Times you should have protected me, but instead, you shouted at me. Why did you do that?" and the little voice trembled.

The Oracle's soothing voice entered the conversation. "Little Lyra, do not be hurt, do not be sad. The older you, who is with me now, had no idea how hurtful her words were to you, her Inner Child." The Oracle put her hands gently onto Lyra's head and spoke again saying, "You should apologise to the small child within you Lyra, the hurt child who is speaking to you now. If you do this with your whole heart, the hurt will begin to fade and you will begin to heal."

Lyra's eyes filled with tears realising what she had done and apologised for hurting her younger self so many times. "I am so sorry, I just didn't know. I said hurtful things without thinking, I didn't know what to do. I didn't realise I was hurting the small child within, I didn't know there was a small child within. Will you please forgive me?" The timid little voice changed into one that sounded braver and stronger. "Yes my older self, I do forgive you, you didn't know any better. I understand now."

Lyra opened her eyes and looked at The Oracle who was smiling kindly at her. "Wow Annie!" Lyra said wiping away tears, "I never imagined I would actually meet my Higher Self and then my younger self. Now I can practise meditating and staying connected to make better choices." The Oracle looked over at Lyra and gave her a knowing look. "Your younger self yearned for understanding and you gave it to her Lyra."

She put the drum to one side and stretched out her arms and legs. "I believe you have heard enough for now. I also know you are feeling rather tired. You may rest and go home when you are ready." Lyra felt a weight had been lifted but wasn't ready to leave her new friends yet. "But Annie, there's no time here, I could stay as long as I wanted and when I got home it would still be the morning I left out, wouldn't it?" The Oracle agreed. "Laeh and Dimaryp said I can come to Airumel again, can I Annie?"

The Oracle put her hand comfortingly on Lyra's hand and told her she was welcome to return whenever she wished. "This world is new to you Lyra, you have only seen a small part of it. There are many more things to see and learn and you may see them at any time, just not now, you need time to reflect." The Oracle realised Lyra had responded deeply to the meditation, so she asked if maybe a rest was what she needed most. "Yes, I think I would like to rest for a while Annie," Lyra decided.

The Oracle took Lyra into a room at the back of the treehouse and showed her an area that was covered in beautiful woven fabrics, she sat down. "Rest your Soul Lyra, we can talk again after. I will be with Doobey when he wakes. You **will** dream, try and remember all of it." Lyra thanked The Oracle and watched as she returned to the balcony and back to Doobey.

Chapter Twelve   Lyra understands the Power Within

She looked around the room. It was just how she had imagined it would be. The pale blue interior had been carved out of the actual trunk. Hand sketched drawings were hanging from knobbles or standing upright on beautifully crafted shelves. Most were of unusual plants, others were of animals. There were what appeared to be rugs made from woven feathers covering the floor, giving the interior a cosy feeling. To the side of her was a large table full of The Oracle's work and next to them a basket containing vegetables.

Lyra yawned, lay down and closed her eyes. For a while she heard the sound of birds and the gentle rustling of the leaves above her, she felt safe and calm, so very happy this wonderful place had found them. It seemed silly, but it was as though she already knew Airumel, or knew the feeling of it anyway. She smiled to herself then drifted off into a deep sleep.

While Lyra was sleeping she **did** have a dream. It was about a street that was full of very narrow houses and there were doors everywhere she looked. Each house had a front door, but there were more doors and Lyra could not understand why. These other doors were in the roofs of the houses and then doors appeared in trees that sprang out of nowhere.

Lyra saw herself walking down the street. She felt as though she was looking for a certain door. Eventually, she came to the end of the street and saw the door she felt sure she had been looking for. It was covered with the most fascinating painting of Nature, and at the top, the Sun was shining brightly. Lyra knew this was the door she wanted to enter and she was just about to push it open, when she awoke.

She sat up and rubbed her eyes. Pushing back the cover she yawned and looked around. It was still light and she'd been in Airumel for what seemed like ages. She thought about Doobey, wondering if he was awake when he wandered in. "Hiya Doobey, you're awake!" she said, holding her hand out to touch him. Doobey barked and trotted over to Lyra. He rubbed his nose on Lyra's leg, then licked her hand. "I just had a very strange dream Doobey," she told him, "What have you been doing?"

Doobey barked again and told Lyra that he'd been playing a game with The Oracle. "I had a thought, Annie guessed what it was. Annie had a thought, I guessed what it was," he said. "Can you do that Doobey?" she giggled. "Yes, she was thinking about the view from the balcony, then she was thinking about a big gathering they are having," he replied. Lyra smiled, still amazed that Doobey could speak. The Oracle appeared at the doorway, and asked, "Did you sleep well Lyra?"

* * * * *

After finishing a bowl of soup, Lyra spoke about her dream. "Well Lyra, the dream has confirmed what has already been said. Also, opening a door in a dream, or a door starting to open, is a symbol of personal growth. It is time to enjoy new opportunities." Lyra smiled, "Yes Annie, I definitely will," she said. "Who are you **now** Lyra, at this moment, do you know that?" Lyra stroked Doobey affectionately as she thought long and hard about The Oracle's question.

After a while she sat forward, cleared her throat and said, "I am an almost teenager, who loves everything, hurts nothing and tries to accept what can't be changed. Until today, I felt that was like a curse, but now I can see it's a blessing. It has given me a whole new outlook on life." Lyra looked at The Oracle who was nodding slowly, listening intently. She reached out and touched Lyra's forehead and said, "That is a powerful way to be, you are blessed my child. NEVER change who you are."

Lyra got up, went outside to the balcony and looked out across the countryside. "I thought it would be going dark by now, I seem to have been in your world all day." The Oracle laughed as she joined Lyra and said, "We have no night time here Lyra, we have no moon or stars either, like you do on the surface." Lyra looked confused, "When do you go to bed then, or don't you need to sleep?" The Oracle answered, "We take, what do they call it in your world ... ah yes, catnaps, we take catnaps when we feel to." Lyra nodded as she pulled on her, now dry trainers.

She followed The Oracle back inside and watched as she continued sketching a landscape she had begun, "Why are most of the things in Airumel, why are their names spelt backwards?" The Oracle turned to Lyra, "You see Lyra, life on the surface is lived very backwardly. It is lived against the forces of Nature, so human's lives are backward. When you live alongside Nature, accepting and respecting **all** life forms, life becomes harmonious. We spell most things the opposite way, because most things here **are** the opposite way.

Noils are a good example, you have seen how gentle they are, even gentler than tibbars." Lyra jumped in, "Rabbits! Lions, sorry noils, are gentler than rabbits, I mean tibbars?" The Oracle laughed heartily and Lyra laughed too, "Yes Lyra, noils are gentler than tibbars, but the Sun Goddess plant that you met, is an exception. There are no plants on the surface even slightly similar."

"When I was with the children," Lyra began, "Dimaryp told me that life on the surface has been changed by hidden secrets. They didn't really tell me what that meant. Can you tell me Annie?" The Oracle's face suddenly changed, it looked serious and determined. She sat for a while in some kind of trance, staring out into the distance. Lyra was about to apologise, thinking she had upset The Oracle, when she spoke.

"Lyra my child, you are very wise and well ahead of your years in understanding. I am not sure you will understand what I am about to tell you though." The Oracle put her sketching to one side, made herself comfortable and continued. "There was a war on the surface many of your Earth years ago. A lot of people lost their lives because of greed and a want to control others. We who live inside the Earth escaped, and found safety and abundance here in Airumel, and the other cities like Airumel." She paused again.

Lyra moved closer to The Oracle, sensing she was telling a story of great distress. "Earth was such a wonderful place to live on Lyra. Everyone lived and loved and cared and shared with each other. There was no judgment or name calling about anyone or anything. One day it all changed, a few people had decided they wanted to control the Earth, so, devised a plan and began to take over.

They made up a terrible lie which caused some humans, to be blamed for everything that ever went wrong. We were hunted and hated. It was very bad, so many people were dying. We had to get out. Once we had made that decision, the Earth became our guide and showed us the way to Inner Earth. Animals helped us and even large birds carried some of us to the opening, to escape."

Lyra felt The Oracle's hurt deeply and tears rolled down her cheeks as she asked, "Is that what the silver bound book in the Green Sanctuary is all about?" The Oracle smiled at Lyra, putting her arm around her and said, "Yes my dear, that tells the whole story. There were people from other islands who empathised with our situation and wished to escape with us, so they came too. We have all been living here peacefully for a very long time, as we did on Earth, before the war."

Lyra wiped her face and blew her nose. She could see the truth about the Earth now and she did understand, in a way she had never known before. She sat for a while thinking about what it must have been like back then, and how important it is for everyone to help the Earth, and mankind, to return to the wonderful state of honour and glory it once was.

* * * * *

The Oracle prepared Lyra and Doobey a juice made from different fruits and suggested after that, they should leave. "We all love having you here, be sure of that. Laeh and Dimaryp were overjoyed by the things you learnt so quickly. The children who you met, felt genuinely upset when you left them, they had wanted to show you and ask you, so many things. Ybur expressed a particular delight in meeting you Lyra but, it is your wellbeing I am thinking of." Lyra realised The Oracle must have been in contact with them all.

Chapter Thirteen   Returning to the Light

Lyra looked at Doobey and Doobey looked back at her. She sighed, "I suppose you're right." She knew they would have to leave Airumel sooner or later. "You can both return at any time," The Oracle told her, "you have the higher energy needed to be part of this world." Lyra was very pleased to hear this. "Maybe we **should** go home then. My mind does feel a little full," she said reluctantly. The Oracle agreed, she needed more rest after experiencing so many new and unusual things.

"When you feel to return Lyra, all you have to do is concentrate on being here." The Oracle put a small, smooth crystal in Lyra's hand and said, "Sit quietly where you are not likely to be disturbed, and hold this crystal against your head, between your eyebrows." Lyra smiled happily, looking at the crystal intently, "and it will work Annie, will it? We'll just be here, but where? Whereabouts Annie? ... Annie??"

Everything started to go hazy. The sounds she had heard that day began running through her head. The children's beautiful song, the ringing of the Tibetan bowls, SG's dainty words, The Oracle's voice and the drumbeats, it all echoed in Lyra's head. The treehouse became a multitude of swirling colours, filling the air and blurring Lyra's vision ... then everything went dark. She closed her eyes.

After a moment, Lyra opened her eyes and looked around, expecting to see Doobey and The Oracle again. It was still dark and she still couldn't see a thing. What's happening, she asked herself. She blinked a few times and began shouting, "Doobey!! Annie!!" Lyra felt around for Doobey, "Doobey? Doobey!! Annie!!? She couldn't find him and she couldn't see The Oracle. "Doobey!!? .... Doobey!!!"

* * * * *

Suddenly Lyra's bedroom door opened, dad switched on the light and walked towards her. "What's wrong Lyra, why are you shouting Doobey? You know he sleeps downstairs." Lyra was looking at her bed in disbelief, then around her bedroom, "What, where's Doobey? Is he okay?" Lyra asked anxiously, amid a muddle of questions flying around in her head. "Doobey's fine Lyra. He **was** fast asleep, he came in to us when he heard you shouting."

Dad sat on the bed and put his hand across Lyra's forehead, "We thought you were sickening for something when you returned home so quickly this morning. You have been asleep for hours. Don't you remember? You do seem rather confused Lyra, what's bothering you?" Lyra **was** confused and wanted to tell her dad all about the awesome day they'd just had, but didn't know where to begin. She sighed. She knew it would be impossible to convince anyone to believe a story like that.

She wanted to be alone and gather her thoughts. She sighed again, "I'm okay dad, I'll go back to sleep in a while. I had the most wonderful day today and I want to think about it all for a while." This time dad looked confused, but he kissed Lyra goodnight and said, "Okay Lyra, if you're sure you feel well, but if you feel ill in the night, come and tell us." He switched off the light and went back downstairs.

Lyra sat up feeling comforted, but bewildered and thought for a while. She switched on her bedside lamp, this time noticing she was wearing her pyjamas. What!! How is this possible? She remembered everything in so much detail. I have definitely missed the day, she thought. Lyra looked at the clock, it said nine thirty. Why don't I remember coming home, this morning?? Or going to bed? I can't remember any of it. Was I dreaming? She sighed yet again.

Suddenly Lyra remembered the crystal The Oracle had given her, and sprang out of bed. She looked around the room eagerly for the proof she needed. Under the bed, in the wardrobe, on the shelves, and the windowsill, but it wasn't there. The clothes she had been wearing that day, were lying in a pile on the floor. Maybe I put it in my pocket, she told herself, anxiously searching each pocket, but found no crystal. The disappointment Lyra felt hurt her head. She slumped backwards onto the bed, but as she did so, felt something press into her back.

She pulled down the covers excitedly and there in front of her eyes was the crystal. Gasping with delight, Lyra grabbed the crystal and looked at it closely. It was the smooth, oval stone The Oracle had given her. The same pale yellow crystal she had seen, only a few minutes earlier. "I knew it! I knew I wasn't dreaming," she said, lowering her voice, then she heard Doobey.

"Lyra you weren't dreaming, we did have the best adventure yet and I brought you home, this morning." Lyra giggled and then remembered. Of course, it makes sense now, in Airumel there is no time … and after storing the crystal safely, she lay back down and went to sleep.

The Oracle

Printed in Great Britain
by Amazon